MINI QUILTS

FROM

TRADITIONAL DESIGNS

MINI QUILTS

FROM
TRADITIONAL DESIGNS

ADELE CORCORAN
CAROLINE WILKINSON

ILLUSTRATIONS BY PENNY BROWN
PHOTOGRAPHS BY SANDRA LOUSADA

Museum Quilts

Published by Museum Quilts (UK) Inc.
254-258 Goswell Road, London EC1V 7EB

The authors have endeavoured to ensure that all project instructions are accurate. However, due to variations in readers' individual skill and materials available, neither the authors nor the publishers can accept responsibility for damages or losses resulting from the instructions herein. All instructions should be studied and clearly understood before beginning any project.

Editors: Ljiljana Ortolja-Baird and Annlee Landman
Designer: Edward Harbour

A CIP catalogue record for this book is available from the British Library

ISBN: 1-897954-55-7

Printed & bound by ORIENTAL PRESS, (DUBAI).

CONTENTS

Introduction

This book was designed for those of us with big ideas and little time. For experts and beginners alike, there are numerous advantages of 'working small'. In a busy world where there is such competition for our leisure time, small quilts, by virtue of their size are attractive projects to pick up, even when you only have a few minutes. Small quilts are quick to cut out and piece, and offer a welcome opportunity to complete a project within a short time, while retaining all the challenges of a larger quilt.

With small quilts, not only can you explore different patterns and learn many techniques in a manageable format, but you can also experiment with design and colour. Your small quilt can be a working model or 'study' for a larger quilt to be made in the future. In this way, it is analogous to an apprentice's master sample; a way to gain confidence in your own sewing skills without a huge investment of time and money. From a practical point of view, small quilts also give you a chance to use up scraps and leftovers from other projects.

The seventeen small quilts in this book are based on classic, time-honoured quilt treasures. They are divided into four categories: Traditional, Appliqué, Amish and Mennonite, and Scrap Quilts. You can make up the quilts exactly as they are shown or change them to suit your needs. Add additional blocks for a crib quilt, borders to make a larger quilt or even scale up the block pattern if you wish. Substitute a different choice of colours for your own interpretation.

Read the Techniques section carefully. It will guide you through the various stages of quilt construction from choosing your fabric to accurate piecing, and finally signing your name. Detailed instructions and illustrations of modern methods are included, along with a section entitled '...especially for small quilts' which highlights important techniques when sewing small.

All the general quiltmaking techniques are the same for small quilts as for large, only more refined and condensed. If you can tackle the accuracy and precision needed to make a small quilt, making larger quilts will become child's play. The disciplines you acquire will transform the way in which you approach quiltmaking in the future.

If you have often found yourself saying, 'Someday, I would really like to make ...' but have never found the time, why not give one a try?

TECHNIQUES

ALL ABOUT FABRIC

Choosing your fabric

Three factors are important when choosing fabric for small quilts: quality, colour and pattern. While speciality fabrics such as velvets and silks have their place, especially in crazy quilts, we recommend dress-weight 100% cotton. Quality, colourfast cottons will stand up to high water and iron temperatures, will hold a crease, will not fray easily and will not allow wadding to 'beard', or seep through to the front.

If you choose loosely woven fabric, first stabilise it with a fusible, light-weight interfacing. This can be done in two ways:
1. Cut out the finished-size shapes from the interfacing, then iron them onto your fabric. Add the seam allowance all around the shape as you cut.
2. Iron large pieces of interfacing to a piece of fabric and cut out the finished-size shapes. Use buttonhole stitch to appliqué to the background fabric.

Your fabric choices will determine the success of a quilt, especially in these small-scale projects. The simplest quilts will come alive because of carefully considered colour and pattern choices. Ultimately, there is only one rule for colour: choose colours you like and that you can live with. Colour selection is a matter of personal choice – there is really no right or wrong and there are no strict rules to follow.

Small quilts have minimal fabric requirements. In the interest of economy, start a scrap bag of fabric remnants. If you intend to mix old and new fabrics within a quilt, inspect the old fabrics thoroughly to ensure they are strong and intact. Use fabrics of equal weight to avoid uneven wear. Try to build a collection that includes prints of varying scales, woven stripes, plaids and solids in a wide range of colours. Keep in mind that very tiny prints are often read as solids but look softer. Colours should vary in value, from light to dark, and in their intensity. Collect gradations of colour in prints and solids to add richness and depth to your colour schemes.

Fabric preparation

For best results, most quilters pre-wash fabrics before sewing. While most fabrics today are colourfast, some of the darker, more vivid colours can bleed. Washing also softens the fabric by removing the sizing and chemicals used in manufacturing, and allows shrinkage to occur. Separate dark and light colours and wash with a small amount of mild liquid soap in hot water. Continue to rinse, until the water is clear. Dry the fabric until slightly damp, then straighten by gently pulling on opposite corners until adjacent sides are at right angles. Press the fabric squares.

Fabric grain

Before cutting your fabric, familiarise yourself with several fabric terms and characteristics. Selvages are the densely woven finished edges of the fabric. Grain is the direction of the threads in the fabric. Crosswise grain runs at right angles to the selvages and is slightly stretchy. Lengthwise grain runs parallel to the selvages and has little stretch. The bias runs at a 45° angle to the selvages and has the maximum stretch.

Cutting

Small quilts leave little margin for error, so measure accurately, mark clearly and cut carefully following grain lines indicated on the templates. Quilters can increase the speed and accuracy of making straight cuts by using a rotary cutter with a self-healing cutting mat, transparent ruler, set square and triangle.

Preparing your fabric for cutting

Fold the fabric in half lengthwise, match selvages and lay on a flat surface. Straighten the raw edges of the fabric by lining up one short side of a 90° triangle with the folded edge. Place a long quilter's ruler along the other short edge of the triangle and trim along the ruler. Now, cut selvages off evenly.

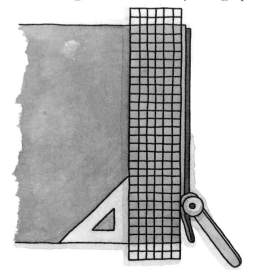

Cutting strips

To cut strips with scissors, measure and mark the desired widths parallel to one of the grain lines. Pin the folded fabric together to prevent shifting, and carefully cut on the marked lines.

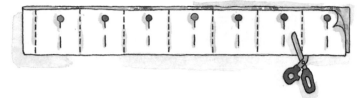

To rotary cut, place the prepared fabric on a cutting mat, with the fold and bulk of the fabric to your right, and the trimmed edge to your left. Measure and cut from the trimmed edge. Hold the transparent quilter's ruler firmly with the left hand and cut with the right (reverse these instructions if you are left-handed). Align the vertical measuring lines on the ruler with the trimmed edge. Move the ruler across the fabric, from left to right, cutting strips to the desired width.

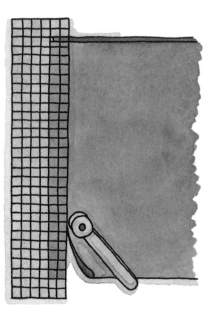

To cut bias strips, find the true bias by aligning one short side of a 90° triangle to the crosswise grain edge of the fabric. Place a long ruler along the diagonal edge of the triangle and cut. Measure the desired width of strips along this diagonal and cut parallel to the diagonal edge.

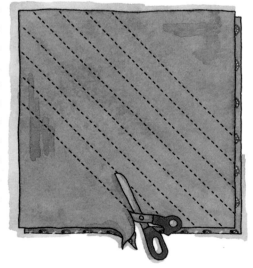

Making and using templates

To make a template, accurately trace the shape onto graph paper or directly onto template plastic. Use a ruler to keep lines straight and all corners square. If you are using the graph paper method, you will need to mount the paper pattern on cardboard before cutting out the shape. Cut out the template carefully, just inside the pencil line. One millimetre (or a fraction of an inch) can make all the difference when working on a small scale. Identify and label each pattern piece along with any placement instructions and grain line arrows.

Templates can be reproduced by photocopying, but will be distorted unless you are able to lay the book perfectly flat on the copier. Centre the pattern in the copier field and make all the copies you will need at one time. Check the first and final copies to make sure they are a true measure.

Piecing templates: For machine-piecing, trace the template and cut out on the solid line. The broken line indicates the sewing line. Trace around the template, placed right side up, on the wrong side of the fabric. Make sure grain arrows are aligned with the fabric grain. Trace each piece close to the next so that fabric is not wasted. Cut out the shapes, exactly on the marked lines, with sharp scissors. For hand-piecing, trace and cut out templates on the broken line to make the finished-sized template. Add seam allowances by eye as you cut.

Appliqué templates: Trace and cut out templates on the single solid line. Place the template right side up, on the right side of the fabric and trace. Leave $^{1}/_{2}$ inch / 1.3 cm between pieces. The pencil line will serve as a guide when turning under your seam allowance. Add a scant $^{1}/_{4}$ inch / 6 mm seam allowance around each piece as you cut.

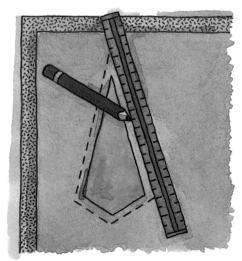

Quilting templates: Trace and cut out on the broken lines. Cut out interior areas for the complete quilting pattern.

Seam allowances

The standard seam allowance for quiltmaking is $^1/_4$ inch / 6 mm. For appliqué, a scant $^3/_{16}$–$^1/_4$ inch / 5–6 mm seam allowance is used depending on the technique. Seam allowances should be trimmed down to $^1/_8$ inch / 3 mm after sewing to eliminate bulk.

Pressing

Pressing is an integral part of quiltmaking, from piecing the block to putting finished blocks together. Pressing keeps your work flat so that it moves under the presser foot easily. As a general rule, press seams towards the darker fabric to avoid a dark shadow showing through to the front. If this is not possible, trim down the seam allowance of the darker fabric narrower than the light one. Press seam allowances in opposite directions to help distribute bulk, but also to allow opposing seams to butt and lock together to form perfect intersections.

Hand-piecing

Hand-piecing is particularly suited for making small quilts as there is greater control in fitting small shapes together so they match perfectly at the seams. It also allows for precision sewing at a relaxed pace. Place two pieces of fabric, right sides together, and pin at right angles to the sewing line, matching corners and stitching lines. Starting with a backstitch, sew on the marked line with small, even running stitches. Turn your work over periodically to check that your stitches are staying on the pencil line. Begin and end each seam at the pencil lines, and not the edge of the fabric. Leave seam allowances free. Finish your seam with another

backstitch. Trim the seam allowances down to $^1/_8$ inch / 3 mm after checking for accuracy.

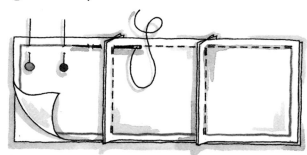

Machine-piecing

Machine-piecing is fast and gives a strong seam. But since there is no marked sewing line on these pieces, it is very important to establish an exact $^1/_4$ inch / 6 mm seam allowance for your sewing machine. Sew a test piece as follows:

1. Cut three strips of fabric 1 × 8 inches / 2.5 × 20.3 cm long. Sew the strips together with $^1/_4$ inch / 6 mm seams.

2. Press the seam allowances in one direction and measure the centre strip. It should be exactly $^1/_2$ inch / 1.3 cm wide.

3. If it is not, use graph paper ruled in $^1/_4$ inches or centimetres to find an exact $^1/_4$ inch / 6 mm sewing line on the throat plate and mark with several layers of masking tape.

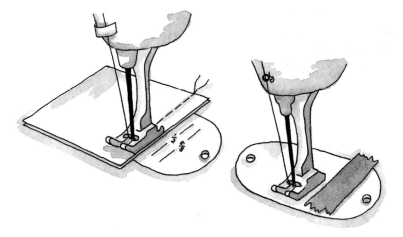

4. Alternatively, use a special presser foot that indicates an exact $^1/_4$ inch / 6 mm seam.

To machine-piece, set the stitch length at 12-15 stitches per inch / 2.5 cm. Following piecing diagrams, place two pieces of fabric right sides together and feed under the needle. Check that the two layers of fabric feed through the machine evenly and without shifting. Pin only if necessary, at right angles to the sewing line. Remove pins just before sewing over them to keep from dulling your needle.

When sewing identical units together, use 'chain-piecing'. Feed the pieces under the presser foot, one after the other, without backstitching, cutting threads, or raising the presser foot. The chain of units will be attached to each other by a short twist of thread, and can then be cut apart.

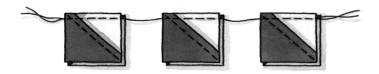

Foundation-piecing

With this method, fabric pieces are sewn onto a base of paper, fabric or stabiliser. Piecing on a foundation lets you make sharp, detailed blocks using tiny fabric scraps. The foundation can then be torn away or left in to provide stability. This method is used for the *Crazy Quilt*, *Courthouse Steps* and *Lemoyne Star* projects.

Quick-piecing

Quick-piecing techniques shorten the time it takes to sew individual pieces, but more importantly, increase the accuracy of stitching small units for tiny quilts.

Eight bi-coloured squares (the sides of the bi-coloured squares will be on the straight of the grain) Cut an equal number of squares of each colour, then mark both diagonals with a pencil on the lighter squares only. Mark another set of intersecting lines through the

centre, this time parallel to the sides. Pin one square of each colour together, with right sides facing. Stitch $1/4$ inch / 6 mm on each side of the diagonal lines. Press to set the stitching, taking extra care not to stretch the square. Cut the square first along the diagonals and then on the quarter square markings. Press open to produce eight bi-coloured squares.

Four bi-coloured squares: This is a very accurate way to make bi-coloured squares measuring less than $1 1/2$ inches / 3.8 cm. Cut an equal number of light and dark squares. If squares are cut along the straight grain of fabric, the resulting four bi-coloured squares will have bias edges. If squares are cut along the bias (diagonal) grain of the fabric, the resulting four bi-coloured squares will have sides on the straight grain. On squares of the lighter colour only, mark the diagonals. Measure and mark a $1/4$ inch / 6 mm seam allowance around the perimeter of the square. Pin squares of each colour together, right sides facing. Sew on the pencil line around the sides of the square. Pivot the needle at each corner, without sewing into the seam allowances. Cut each square apart on the diagonal lines only. Press open to form four bi-coloured squares.

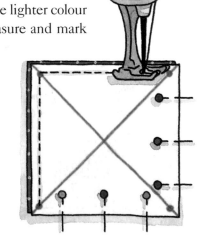

Bias strip-piecing: This technique is useful if you have bias strips left over from cutting other pieces. Prepare a square template, including seam allowances, of the correct size. Cut bias strips from each colour $1/4$ inch / 6 mm wider than the diagonal measure of the template square. Square the fabric, then use a right angle triangle and a quilter's ruler to mark the bias cutting lines on each of the two fabrics. Pin a strip of each colour together and sew. Press strips open, with seams towards the darker colour. Align the diagonal line of the template directly over the seam joining the bias strips. Trace around the template, and cut out the squares.

Strip-piecing: Cut strips ½ inch / 1.3 cm wider than the finished measurement required. Sew strips together using a ¼ inch / 6 mm seam allowance. This multi-striped length of fabric can then be cut into bands of varying widths to form squares or rectangles. Assorted strips sewn together may be used to form random pieced borders, such as those in *Kate's House*. Strips sewn together in a specific colour sequence are necessary for designs such as *Trip Around the World*.

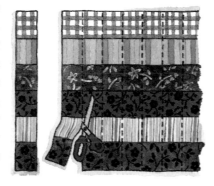

APPLIQUÉ

This is a technique of layering or applying one piece of fabric onto another, with a blind hem stitch. Appliqué should have smooth curves, crisp points and corners and barely visible stitching. We have used four of the different methods of appliqué in this book.

Needle-turning

Arrange the appliqué shapes on the background fabric. Baste in place through the centre to allow you to turn under an ⅛ inch / 3 mm seam allowance without having to remove any basting stitches. A light dab from a fabric glue stick will secure tiny shapes to the background fabric. Thread a No. 9 SHARP needle with a single strand of matching thread. Hold the background fabric so that the appliqué piece is close to you, and stitch on the edge farthest away from you, using a blind hem

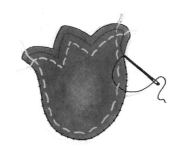

stitch. Work your stitches from right to left if you are right-handed (reverse direction if you are left-handed). Bring the needle up through the background fabric, catching a few threads of the folded appliqué edge. Insert the needle back down through the background fabric, a fraction above the spot where it came up, and move the needle a scant ⅛ inch / 3 mm away for the next stitch. Keep the stitches snug but not so tight that they pucker the edge of the appliqué. Use the tip of your needle to turn under short sections along the pencil line as you go. Finger press the seam allowance under. For convex curves, use your needle to turn under the seam allowance only a stitch or two at a time. Finger press, and at the same time give the edge a slight stretch. This may be enough to curve and stitch the seam without having to clip it. At the end of a thread, take a backstitch and knot the thread from the back of your work. Remove the basting stitches after all the appliqué pieces have been sewn.

Pre-basting

Turn under and baste the ¼ inch / 6 mm seam allowance on the pencil line using a running stitch. Do not turn under edges that will be covered by other pieces of appliqué. On tight curves or at acute angles, trim or clip into seam allowances slightly. Take special care when turning a sharp point to finger press the seam allowance all around on the pencil line. With the wrong side up, turn the right side seam allowance over and hold between the thumb and forefinger. Now bring the left side seam allowance over the right. Baste with two tiny stitches. Repeat with all other points. Arrange pre-basted shapes on the background fabric and pin in place.

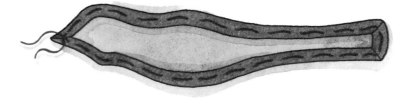

Using a blind hem stitch, sew up to a point as instructed in the first method, then take two tiny stitches to anchor the point firmly.

With scissors, grade some of the excess seam allowance at the point. Tuck under any remaining seam allowance with the point of your needle, and continue stitching to the next point.

Machine appliqué

Using the special stitches on your sewing machine, you can finish off appliqué shapes without turning under the raw edges. Use a smooth satin stitch to bind the edge to the background. You can also use a decorative embroidery stitch, such as a buttonhole stitch, spaced no more than $^1/8$ inch / 3 mm apart on fine cotton and $^1/4$ inch / 6 mm apart on thick woollens or felt.

Iron-on interfacing

With this method, leaves and small circles for berries and flower centres are simple to make. Cut a circle the desired finished diameter from iron-on interfacing. Iron onto the wrong side of the fabric. Cut out the shape, adding a scant $^1/4$ inch / 6 mm seam allowance. Run a single row of gathering stitches around the circle about $^1/8$ inch / 3 mm from the edge and leave enough excess thread at the start and finish to gather. Overlap the stitching at the beginning and end. Now pull the threads gently, distributing the gathers evenly. The interfacing will help define the circle and the gathered seam allowance will slightly pad the shape. Finger press lightly, pin in place on the background fabric and appliqué with a blind hem stitch.

SETTING THE BLOCKS

Blocks can be laid out in four ways: **straight**, as in *Bluebird*; **on point**, as in *Basket of Chips* and *Tulips*; **medallion** or in **strips**. In a straight setting, blocks are laid out parallel to the sides of the quilt top. Blocks on point are set on the diagonal. Medallion quilts have a central motif surrounded by ever-increasing frames. Strippy quilts are made up of pieced or plain strips in top to bottom stripes. Each of these basic settings can be altered by adding plain or pieced sashing (strips of fabric used to frame or join blocks) and by alternating pieced or appliqué blocks with plain blocks.

Arrange the blocks to your liking, pinning and labelling them so that you can sew them together in sequence, according to your design. When joining blocks into rows, and when joining rows of blocks together, take special care to match seams exactly. This is easy to achieve if you press the seam allowances in opposite directions on alternate rows. If any of the seams do not match neatly, ease or gently stretch the fabric to fit.

If you change a quilt from its recommended setting, draw up a plan on graph paper to determine which dimensions will change. Be sure to adjust the sashing and border dimensions accordingly.

BORDERS

Borders both contain and frame the designs used to make up the quilt top. They are a resting place for your eyes and a definite boundary that leads the eye back to the centre of the quilt. The planning and piecing of the borders should be given much time and thought. Borders can add variety, interest and balance without competing with the main body of the quilt. Measurements for cutting border strips accompany the projects, but should you wish to modify the designs, take care to measure the quilt first through the centres and then on each side to find the length to cut your strips.

Always cut border strips $^1/2$ inch / 1.3 cm wider than the finished width you have chosen. As a rule, pin then sew border strips on, starting at the centre and working outwards. To ensure a smooth, flat border, take care not to stretch either border strips or the quilt top while sewing. Also, border strips for the top and bottom should be the same length, as should the two border strips for the sides.

Square-end borders

Measure the width of the quilt at the top and bottom, and add one inch/2.5 cm for seams and ease of handling. Using these measurements, cut two strips. To determine the length to

cut the side borders, measure the length of each side of the quilt and add the width of the top and bottom borders, plus one inch/ 2.5 cm for seams and ease of handling. Fold each border in half to find the centre, and lightly crease. With right sides facing and centrepoints matching, pin border strips to the quilt, working from the centre out to each corner. Sew border strips first to the top and

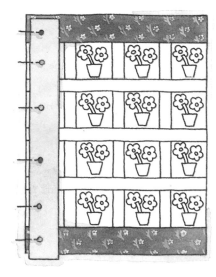

bottom. Press out, then sew remaining strips to the sides. Seams are normally pressed towards the border. However, if you intend to quilt-in-the-ditch, press seam allowances away from that edge to reduce the number of layers you must quilt through.

Mitred borders

Cut each border strip to measure the length of one of the sides, plus twice the border width plus 3 inches/7.62 cm for seams and ease of handling. Working from the centre out to each corner, pin the border strips to each side so that the fabric overhangs each end equally. Sew one side at a time with a ¼ inch/6 mm seam allowance, starting and ending ¼ inch/6 mm in from the edge.

Do not sew into the seam allowances. Sew each border strip in the same way. Press the seam towards the border. Lay the quilt out on a flat surface. As illustrated, lay one border strip over the other at each corner. Turn under the top strip at a 45° angle, aligning it accurately with the underneath strip. Press lightly and pin, then

slipstitch in place. On the wrong side, trim each corner seam leaving a ¼ inch/6 mm seam allowance.

PREPARING TO QUILT

Embroidery

Before assembling the quilt layers, you may wish to use embroidery to define outlines, to mark circles and lines too narrow for bias tape, to add detail and texture, and to hide the raw edges of appliqué. It is an important decorative feature on the seams of crazy quilts. We have used chain stitch for the circular outline in the *Pennsylvania Wreath*, satin stitch and french knots for *Bluebird*, and a variety of stitches for the *Crazy Quilt* project.

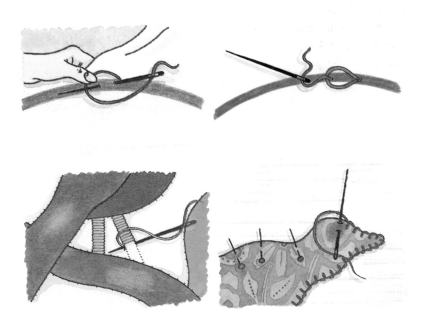

Pressing the quilt top

Cut off all loose threads, front and back. Check that seam allowances are tidy and that unnecessary seam bulk has been trimmed back. Carefully press the quilt top for the last time, first from the back and finally from the front.

Marking the quilt top

Test your marking tools on a fabric scrap to ensure that they will not permanently mark the fabric. Although small quilts will often be examined at close range, very fine lines, covered with tiny, even stitches will almost disappear. Mark the quilt top before assembling the quilt layers. On light coloured fabrics, use a very sharp H or 2H pencil. White or silver pencils or chalk markers will be necessary on dark fabrics. Measure and mark straight lines and grids with a transparent quilter's ruler or straight edge. You can also use pale blue or yellow dressmaker's carbon paper and a tracing wheel for an easy-to-follow quilting guide. Loose chalk marking wheels give a beautiful line, but brush off easily. Marker pens with 'disappearing' ink are available, but the long-term effects on the fabrics are not known. If your quilting pattern has dark, heavy lines, place light coloured fabrics over the pattern and trace directly. You can also trace around a quilting template or stencil. Straight lines can be marked with low-tack, masking tape. Quilt against the edge of the tape and move it as you stitch. Remove the tape from the unfinished quilt as you finish a quilting session. If left on too long, the adhesive will transfer to the fabric. Echo quilting (concentric circles, arcs or lines echoing the original quilting line, pieced or appliquéd shape) can be marked freehand. Outline quilting ($\frac{1}{4}$ inch/6 mm from the seam line) and in-the-ditch quilting (no more than $\frac{1}{8}$ inch/3 mm) need not be marked.

Wadding

There are many excellent waddings available in a variety of fibres: all cotton, cotton/polyester and all synthetic. All are suitable for quiltmaking in general, but for very small quilts, only the thinnest low-loft wadding is recommended. Look for new high-quality wadding that separates easily, into half the original thickness.

Assembling the quilt layers

A well-prepared and basted quilt will help ensure a beautifully smooth result. Pinning and basting can be tedious, but try not to skimp on this step. On a smooth, flat surface, place the backing fabric right side down and anchor with short strips of masking tape at each corner and centre of each side. Next, smooth the wadding onto the backing fabric. Finally centre the pressed and marked quilt top on the wadding, right side up. Backing and wadding should extend approximately 1–1$\frac{1}{2}$ inches/2.5–3.8 cm all around. Pin the layers together at each corner and every 4 inches/10.2 cm. Remove the tape at the corners.

Basting

With the layered quilt still on the flat surface, use a long-threaded darning needle to baste from the centre to each corner and from the centre to each side. Then, baste a 1$\frac{1}{2}$–2 inch/3.8–5.1 cm grid over the entire quilt with large stitches. Finally, to protect the edges from fraying while quilting, enclose the excess wadding by folding and basting the raw edge of the backing over the quilt top.

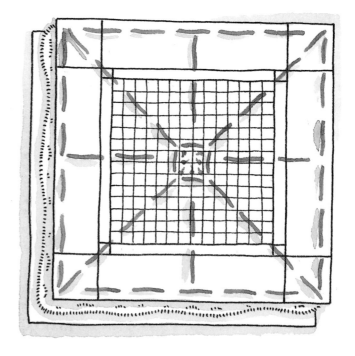

QUILTING

The primary purpose of quilting is to secure the quilt layers and prevent the wadding from shifting. Never leave large areas unquilted. Partially quilted tops look unfinished, and haphazard stitching may distort the quilt top. Very small quilts can be lap-quilted, but the use of a hoop helps to maintain an even tension and reduces the chance of pulling stitches too tight. You can use a hoop to quilt the edges of your quilt if you first baste lengths of scrap fabric to each unfinished side. Three methods of quilting are suitable for small quilts.

Hand-quilting

A simple running stitch is the basis of all hand-quilting. It is easier to produce a tiny stitch with a No. 8 or 9 BETWEEN needle. Use good quality quilting thread for strength and its slight sheen which enhances the stitches. To help prevent knotting, some quilters run thread through beeswax before quilting. Secure the basted quilt in a hoop to hold it taut and smooth on top and bottom. Resting one side of the hoop on a table, with the other side in your lap, frees both your hands to sew. Wear a thimble on your middle finger, as it is difficult to push the needle through all the layers without one. One hand is used to guide the needle from the front and the other, under the hoop, to feel that the needle has penetrated all the quilt layers. Start in the centre and work out to the edges. Knot the end of the quilting thread, no more than 18 inches / 45.7 cm in length, and stitch into the top two layers of the quilt, coming up through the quilting line. A sharp tug will pull the knot into the middle layer of wadding.

Try at first to make even stitches, about 7–8 per inch / 2.5 cm. Even stitching is more important than the number of stitches per inch / 2.5 cm. Take three or four running stitches.

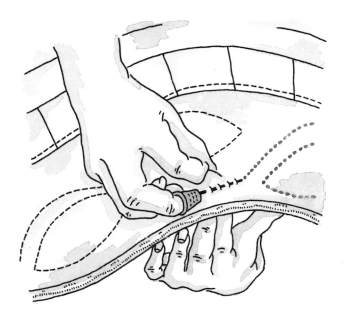

Proficient quilters use a rhythmic rocking motion with their needle hand to quilt smoothly and evenly. To finish off, tie two small knots about $\frac{1}{2}$ and $\frac{3}{4}$ inch / 1.3 and 1.9 cm from the last stitch. Again, run the thread between the layers, into the wadding, for about one inch / 2.5 cm.

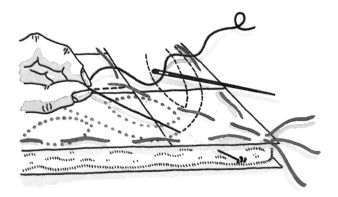

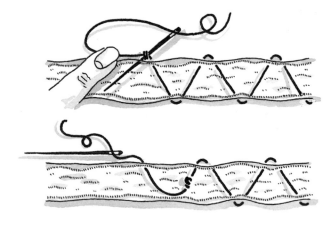

Give a sharp tug to pull the finishing knots through.

Machine-quilting

Prepare a quilt as carefully for machine quilting as for hand quilting. If your machine does not have a walking foot, you will have to baste closely to prevent the backing feeding through the machine faster than the quilt top. Fit your machine with a larger, No. 14 needle. Match the bobbin thread to the backing fabric. Either matching thread or transparent thread works well for the top stitching. Try to work a continuous quilting line, stopping and starting as little as possible. Begin and end in an inconspicuous place. Pull the loose thread ends to the back and finish off each end as in hand-quilting or set the stitch length almost to zero and stitch two or three times in place to secure.

Tying or tufting

This technique is used to fasten the quilt layers together when thick wadding makes traditional quilting impossible. In small quilts, tying is used for decorative purposes and any thread such as wool, 6-strand embroidery cotton, soft linen thread or very narrow ribbon is suitable. Sew on buttons, beads or other embellishments at intervals as well. Plan to put your ties at the same points all over the quilt top, every 2–3 inches/5.1–7.6 cm apart.

On the right side of the quilt top, stab stitch through all layers. Leave 4 inches/10.2 cm of thread on top to tie. Now bring the needle back to the top of the quilt, about ⅛ inch/3 mm from the first stitch. Stab stitch once more down through the first stitch and up through the second stitch. Tie securely in a square knot, right over left, then left over right.

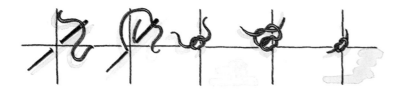

If you choose to sew ribbons to the quilt top, make a tiny bow with a piece of ribbon to determine the length you need for each bow. Cut as many lengths as you will need. From the right side of the quilt top, stab stitch through the ribbon and all quilt layers with a needle and knotted thread. Bring the needle up through the centre of the ribbon.

Repeat with 3 or 4 tiny stitches. Sew the ribbons at intervals across the quilt top. Finish off the stitches with a tiny knot and run the end of the thread between the quilt layers as in ordinary quilting. Any knots on the surface of the ribbon will be hidden when you tie the bow.

Buttons and beads can be sewn on in the usual manner with quilting thread. Using a knotted thread, start with a stitch on top of the quilt, then sew the button on securely, making sure that the thread goes through all three layers with each stitch. Finish off the stitching by running the end between the layers of the quilt for 1–2 inches/2.5–5.1 cm.

BINDINGS

There are three different binding techniques used for the projects in this book. Cut binding strips on the lengthwise grain of the fabric, if possible. If that increases your yardage too much, then cut on the crosswise grain which is slightly stretchier. If binding a quilt with a scalloped or rounded corner, as in *Tulips*, cut binding strips on the crosswise grain or use bias binding.

Continuous, separate binding

In this finishing method, fabric strips are sewn into a continuous length, before being applied to the raw edges of the quilt. Binding width is a personal preference, but most quiltmakers opt for a maximum width of ¾ inch/1.9 cm. Decide what the finished width of your binding will be and multiply that measurement by two. Add ⅛ inch/3 mm to allow for the loft of the wadding plus another ½ inch/1.3 cm for seam allowances. This will be the width of your strips. Now, cut enough binding strips to equal the length of all four sides of the quilt plus 8 inches/20.3 cm for mitres, seam allowances and ease. Sew the strips together, then press the binding in half lengthwise with wrong sides together. Open up the fold, then turn in and press ¼ inch/6 mm of one raw edge to the wrong side. Starting at the centre of the bottom of the quilt, match raw edges of the quilt to the unpressed edge of the binding and pin in place. Fold in the starting edge of the binding ½ inch/1.3 cm. Stitch through all layers, beginning with a backstitch, using a standard ¼ inch/6 mm seam allowance.

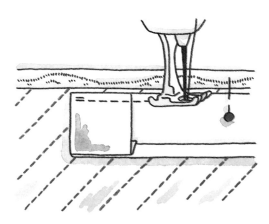

Stop sewing ¼ inch/6 mm away from the first corner, backstitch and clip threads.

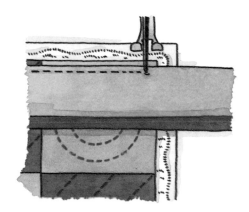

To mitre the corner, fold the binding strip up at a 45° angle, then back down to align it with the adjacent edge of the quilt top. This pleat will give you enough fullness to fit around the corners as you fold the binding around to the back.

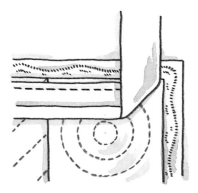

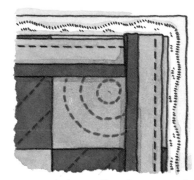

Continue sewing around the quilt edge, stopping to mitre each corner in turn. As you approach the end, allow 1 inch/2.5 cm to overlap the folded-back section where you began. Backstitch at the join. Trim away the excess wadding and backing. Wrap the folded edge of the binding around to the back of the quilt to cover the machine stitches.

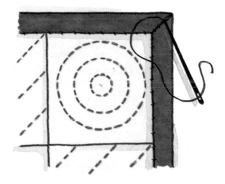

Pin, then slipstitch binding and mitres, front and back, in place.

For a rounded corner, place a spool of thread or small circle template in the corner and trace. Trim the curve carefully with small scissors. Again, follow the directions for continuous, separate binding. Clip into the seam allowance, if necessary, to ease the binding strip around the trimmed corner.

Fold-finishing

In this method, the raw edges of the quilt top and backing fold in on themselves.

Trim the wadding and backing even with the quilt top. Carefully trim wadding back ¼ inch/ 6 mm. Fold the backing over to enclose the wadding. Turn under ¼ inch/6 mm along the edge of the quilt top, and pin to the backing. Using a matching thread, slipstitch along the edge, all the way around the quilt.

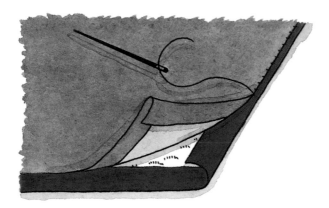

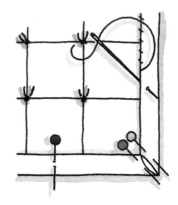

Self-binding

In this method the backing of the quilt wraps around the raw edge of the quilt top to become the binding.

Baste around the edge of the quilt top through all layers and stitch on the seam allowance line. Trim wadding $\frac{1}{4}$ inch / 6 mm from the seam line. Trim backing $\frac{7}{8}$ inch / 2.2 cm from the seam line. Turn down the corner points of the backing to meet the corner seam allowances. Finger press the fold. Trim away the point of the backing on this fold line to reduce the bulk at the corners. Turn under $\frac{1}{4}$ inch / 6 mm of the raw edge of the backing to the wrong side and press lightly. Bring the folded edge of the backing to the front of the quilt and pin. Pin each corner into a neat mitre. Slipstitch the binding to cover the seam line. Remove the basting stitches.

SIGNING YOUR QUILT

The final stitch is taken, the last basting thread removed, but the quilt is not finished until you sign your name and date it. If possible include the town, county and country of origin. If the quilt is a gift, give the name of the recipient and the occasion for which it was made. No amount of information is too much.

There are various ways to sign your quilt.

1. Make your name and date part of the border quilting plan.
2. Use a permanent, fabric marking pen to record details on a square of fabric and appliqué this to the back of the quilt.
3. Cross-stitch the information on cross-stitch fabric or canvas.

Some quilters record detailed information on paper to accompany their quilts. This is a wonderful way to tell future generations about you, the maker, and how you lived and worked. To follow in this tradition, prepare a pocket with either a button or snap fastener, and slipstitch it to the corner of the quilt. Fold and insert the written paper into the pocket. Remember to remove the paper when you wash the quilt.

...especially for small quilts

Take special care when choosing fabrics for miniature and small quilts. Restrict yourself to fabrics with a scale appropriate to the quilt's diminutive size. A large, widely spaced check or bold, floral chintz will be lost when cut into small squares.

It is important to include a variety of tone, colour, scale, and contrast in your fabric selection. Combine small prints, such as pin-dots, small checks, florals and plaids, but make sure to emphasise the contrast between fabrics to help distinguish the small pieces. For instance, if the background and piecing fabrics are too similar in tone, the shapes will blend into one another. On the other hand, if the background fabric is too strong, it will overpower the composition.

If changing block dimensions or designs, always draw up a full-size block plan, preferably on graph paper, to check your measurements before you make templates or cut strips.

Accuracy at all stages of construction is essential for the success of your small quilt. Before starting your project, double check that you have cut your strips and pieces accurately. To make absolutely certain, it is often a good idea to make a sample block. Also, practise sewing a consistent, straight and accurate ¼ inch / 6 mm seam allowance on scrap fabric.

Pins are awkward to use when working with very small pieces, but can be effective to hold seam allowances in place when matching seams. This is necessary for precise intersections. Always pin at right angles to the seam. To avoid bumpy seams and damaged needles, pull the pins out as you sew.

To accommodate the small units, set the stitch length on your sewing machine to 10–12 stitches per inch / 2.5 cm. Remember, it is very difficult to unpick tiny stitches, so try to sew at a controlled and even pace.

Use a seam ripper or a darning needle to feed small fabric pieces under the presser foot.

Use 'assembly line' chain-piecing whenever possible for speed and accuracy. An interesting development of this technique is to begin your chain of pieces by first sewing on a folded scrap of fabric. Continue to stitch, feeding the pieces under the presser foot without lifting it. Cut off the leading scrap and reuse it at the end of your chain. This eliminates untidy thread ends and bobbin jams and reduces the chance of the machine 'chewing up' the small pieces at the beginning of a seam.

After sewing each seam, check that you have accurately joined the appropriate edges, then trim away excess seam allowances to ⅛ inch / 3 mm before sewing the next seam. This will help reduce seam bulk at intersections when putting the block together.

Plan pressing directions before sewing your block to take into consideration your quilting design, to help distribute the bulk, and most importantly, so that you can butt opposing seam allowances against each other to form perfect, accurate intersections. Press frequently and carefully so that your work lies flat and passes under the machine presser foot smoothly. Whenever possible, press seams towards the darker fabric. At junctions where many seams meet, try to press in a circular direction. Only when absolutely necessary, press seams open.

Once you have completed all the blocks for a project, press and measure them, one at a time, to ensure they are all exactly the same size and all true squares. If they are not, gently ease the blocks to fit.

Keep border and binding widths in proportion to the central design of the quilt.

Use only the lightest weight, low-loft wadding or a single layer of standard wadding that you have gently separated in two. If you have difficulty separating the layers, try ironing standard wadding between tea towels.

Use very small hand-quilting stitches in keeping with the scale of the quilt.

Traditional Quilts

Mariner's Compass

Evening Star

Flying Geese

Bow-tie

This old English pattern was taken from the card of a ship's compass and was a favourite of 19th century quiltmakers living on the eastern seaboard of America. With its many narrow, radiating points, this quilt is a perfect project for quilters who enjoy hand-piecing.

MARINER'S COMPASS

Skill level: Advanced

Finished quilt: $17^1/_2 \times 17^1/_2$ inches / 44.5 × 44.5 cm
Finished block: 5 × 5 inches / 12.7 × 12.7 cm
4 inch / 10.2 cm diameter compass
Number of blocks: 9

MATERIALS

- Cream print $^1/_4$ yard / 25 cm
- Assorted yellow prints 9 scraps at least
  3 × 4 inches / 7.6 × 10.2 cm
- Dark green print $^1/_8$ yard / 15 cm
- Assorted red prints $^5/_8$ yard / 60 cm
- Background prints for compass blocks—
  one light and one dark $^1/_4$ yard / 25 cm **each**
- Light brown print $^1/_2$ yard / 50 cm
- Wadding 20 × 20 inches / 50.8 × 50.8 cm
- Backing 20 × 20 inches / 50.8 × 50.8 cm

CUTTING INSTRUCTIONS

✂ Make Templates **A**, **B**, **C**, **D**, and **E** following the instructions in the Techniques section. To mark the fabric for cutting, place the template on the wrong side of the fabric. Trace around each template with a sharp marking pencil. This is your sewing line. Add a scant ¼ inch / 6 mm seam allowance as you cut.

Sawtooth Border

1. Cut the light brown and red print fabrics chosen for the sawtooth border into 18 inch / 45.7 cm squares. Place the two squares on top of each other and cut seven bias strips, 1½ inches / 3.8 cm wide. These strips will be used to quick-piece the half-square triangles of the border. Alternatively, use Template F to cut 60 triangles from each fabric square.

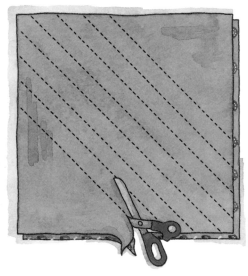

2. For the corners, cut two red squares and two light brown squares, 1½ × 1½ inches / 3.8 × 3.8 cm.

3. For the binding, cut five strips, 1¼ inches / 3.2 cm wide across the remaining width of the light brown fabric.

Compass Blocks

1. Cut out the pieces for one compass at a time. For each, cut four red points with **Template A**, four green points with **Template B**, eight yellow points with **Template C**, and 16 cream wedges with **Template D**.

2. For the two background blocks, cut four squares 5½ × 5½ inches / 14 × 14 cm from the light fabric and five squares the same size from the dark print.

PIECING THE BLOCKS

✂ For the best results, choose sewing thread which exactly matches the fabric being sewn. Once a seam has been sewn, trim the excess seam allowance down to ⅛ inch / 3 mm and press open.

✂ To keep the points sharp, be sure to finish your seam at the very end or tip of the point.

1. Following the diagram, sew a **cream D wedge** to adjacent sides of a **yellow C point**. Repeat this until all eight **D–C–D wedges** have been completed.

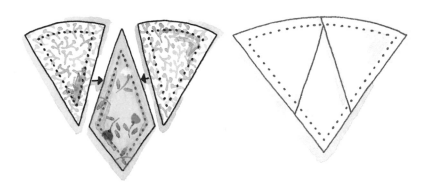

2. Sew a **D–C–D wedge** to each side of four **green B points** until you have made four larger wedges.

3. Make four quarters by sewing an **A point** to the right-hand edge of each wedge made in **Step** 2.

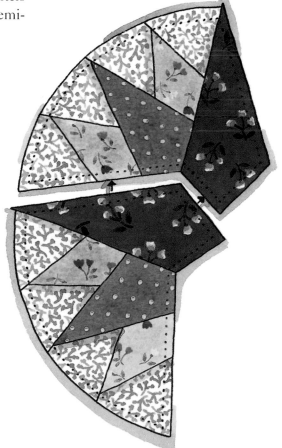

4. Sew the quarters to make two semi-circles.

5. Sew the two semi-circles together to make a full circle as shown.

6. Complete all nine compasses, following the same sequence. Press lightly to encourage the seams to lie flat.

SEWING THE COMPASS TO THE BACKGROUND SQUARE

1. To make it easier to turn under the raw edges of the pieced compass, machine or hand-stitch all around the seam allowance. Use thread colour which exactly matches the fabric used for the **D wedge**.

2. Using the sewn line as a guide, turn under and baste the raw edge of the compass making sure that the stitching does not show on the right side.

3. Find the middle of the background square by folding it in quarters. Centre the compass onto the background square by matching midpoints. Pin and baste the compass in place.

4. Appliqué the compass onto the background square using matching thread and small invisible stitches. Remove any top basting.

5. If you intend to quilt the blocks, reduce the bulk from behind by carefully cutting away the base fabric to ¼ inch / 6 mm.

PUTTING THE BLOCKS TOGETHER

1. Arrange the blocks in three rows with three squares in each row, alternating a dark square with a light one. Pin, then sew the blocks together, pressing seam allowances towards the dark fabric.

2. Join the three rows together to complete the central panel.

ADDING THE BORDERS

1. Stitch red and light brown bias strips of similar length together. Gently press the seams open. Make seven pieced strips.

2. Place **Template E** on the bias strip with the diagonal line over the seam. Mark and cut out a total of 60 squares from the pieced strips.

3. Sew pieced border strips, each with 15 squares, alternating colours to create the sawtooth effect. Press seams towards the darker fabric.

4. Pin, then sew two of the strips to opposite sides of the quilt so that the brown triangles form the outer edge of the quilt.

5. Sew a red square and a brown square to each end of the two remaining strips before attaching them to the top and bottom of the quilt.

QUILTING & FINISHING

1. Press the quilt top carefully. Trim away any loose threads which may show through to the front of the quilt. Because the quilting pattern does not require marking, assemble the quilt layers and baste thoroughly.

2. Quilt in-the-ditch around the red star points. Quilt radiating lines through the centres of the green and yellow points into the background block.

3. Sew binding strips into a continuous length. Use separate binding to finish the raw edges as described in the Techniques section.

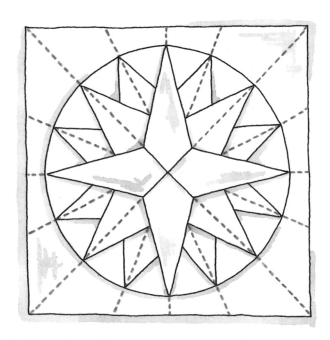

EVENING STAR

The star is one of the oldest and most popular quilt motifs. Also known as *Saw Tooth* and *Ohio Star*, this classic pattern is scaled down to 3 inches/7.6cm. The unusual choice of large-scale pattern in the setting blocks breaks with the conventional rules for small quilts, but provides visual interest and sets off the tiny prints used in the pieced stars. The Indonesian-style fabric used in the border complements the paisley designs beautifully.

EVENING STAR

Skill level: Beginner

Finished quilt: 22 × 22 inches / 55.8 × 55.8 cm
Finished block: 3 × 3 inches / 7.5 × 7.5 cm
Number of blocks: 16

MATERIALS

- ❖ Brown prints 16 scraps, each at least 5 × 5 inches / 12.7 × 12.7 cm
- ❖ Cream fabric ¼ yard / 25 cm
- ❖ Paisley prints 17 scraps, each at least 4 × 4 inches / 10.2 × 10.2 cm
- ❖ Black print for inner border ¼ yard / 25 cm
- ❖ Brown Indonesian print for outer border and binding ½ yard / 50 cm
- ❖ Wadding 25 × 25 inches / 63.5 × 63.5 cm
- ❖ Backing 25 × 25 inches / 63.5 × 63.5 cm

CUTTING INSTRUCTIONS

Brown prints
1. From each of the 16 scraps, cut one square using **Template A** and eight squares using **Template B**.

Cream prints
1. Cut 64 squares using **Template B** and 64 rectangles using **Template C**.

✂ If you would prefer to use the quick-cutting technique instead of templates, cut five strips, 1¼ inches / 3.2 cm wide across the full width of the fabric. Cut the strips down into 64 **B squares**, 1¼ × 1¼ inches / 3.2 × 3.2 cm and 64 **C rectangles**, 1¼ × 2 inches / 3.2 × 5.1 cm.

Paisley prints
1. Cut nine setting squares using **Template D**.

2. Cut 12 side triangles using **Template E**.

3. Cut four corner triangles using **Template F**.

✂ To quick-cut these pieces, make three stacks of pressed fabric scraps, each with three layers. Cut nine setting squares, 3½ × 3½ inches / 8.9 × 8.9 cm. For the side triangles, make two stacks of three scraps each, and cut six squares, 3⅞ × 3⅞ inches / 9.8 × 9.8 cm. Cut in half, along the diagonal. With the remaining two scraps, cut two squares, 3 × 3 inches / 7.6 × 7.6 cm, then cut in half diagonally, to make four corner triangles.

Borders

1. For the inner border, cut two strips, 1¼ inches / 3.2 cm across the full width of the fabric.

2. For the outer border, cut four strips, 2½ inches / 6.4 cm across the full width of the fabric. Cut the strips down to 26 inches / 66 cm. Extra length is given for the corners. Set the leftovers aside for the binding.

Binding

1. Cut each of the four leftover strips in half, lengthwise.

PIECING THE BLOCKS

✂ To make the flying geese units we will be using a quick-piecing technique which does not involve difficult-to-use, small triangles.

1. As a stitching guideline, draw a diagonal line with a marking pencil, on the wrong side of each brown **B square**.

2. With right sides together and raw edges matching place a brown **B square** on top of a cream **C rectangle**.

3. Stitch through both layers, exactly on the pencil line. To keep the points sharp, be careful to stitch through both corners.

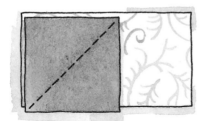

4. Cut away the excess seam allowance to ⅛ inch / 3 mm. Press the brown triangle back over the stitching line to form one side of the flying geese unit.

5. To complete one 'flying geese' unit, repeat the sequence, using a second brown **B square** on the other side of the rectangle. The point of the cream 'goose' triangle should be exactly ¼ inch / 6 mm away from the top raw edge of the rectangle.

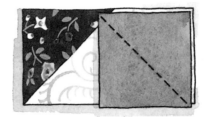 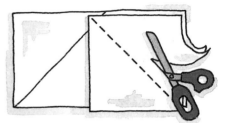

6. Sew a cream **B square** to each short side of two flying geese units. These will make up the top and bottom rows of the block. Press seams to the right.

7. For the middle row, sew a flying geese unit to opposite sides of a centre **A square**. Press seams to the left.

8. Follow the same sequence to make 15 more blocks.

PUTTING THE BLOCKS TOGETHER

1. Lay out the star blocks, the paisley **setting squares**, the **side triangles** and the **corner triangles**. Arrange the blocks so that the colours are balanced and the blocks along the perimeter complement the border fabrics.

2. Pin and sew blocks together in diagonal rows. Begin and end each row with a **side triangle** and alternate star blocks with **setting squares**. Press each row carefully, alternating the pressing direction, to make it easier for the rows to lock together.

3. Sew the diagonal rows together.

4. Complete the central design by adding the four **corner triangles**.

ADDING THE BORDERS

Inner border
1. Cut one strip down into two, the exact length of the sides of the quilt top. Pin, then sew in place. Press the border strips out.

2. Measure the width of the quilt top, including the side borders. Cut the second border strip into two strips to match. Pin, then sew the borders to the top and bottom of the quilt. Press out.

Outer border
1. Pin the strips to opposite sides of the quilt top, allowing several inches/cm of excess fabric to overhang at both ends. Sew the strips onto the quilt, beginning and ending the seam ¼ inch/6 mm from the edges. Press the borders out.

2. Pin the remaining strips to the top and bottom of the quilt, leaving extra fabric to overhang as before. Sew the strips to the quilt, beginning and ending your stitching at the seam of the outer border. DO NOT sew over the side, outer border. Press the borders out.

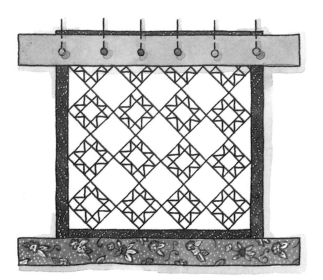

3. To mitre the corner, fold the bottom border strip under at a 45° angle. The excess strip will line up with the excess side border strip. Pin, then press the mitre in place. Use a drafting triangle to check the mitre is square. Slipstitch in place.

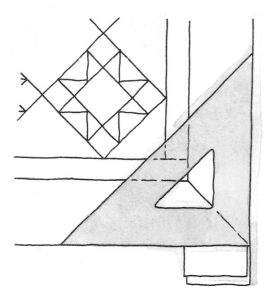

4. Trim away extra border fabric from the back to ¼ inch / 6 mm of the seam. Make sure there are no puckers or gaps.

5. Repeat these steps to mitre the other three corners.

QUILTING & FINISHING

1. Press the quilt top carefully, and trim away any loose threads from the back.

2. Assemble and baste the three quilt layers.

3. Outline quilt the stars and quilt in-the-ditch along the block seams.

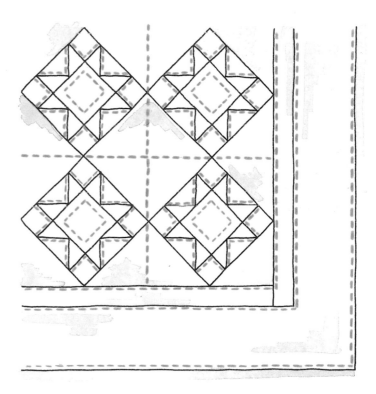

4. Trim away excess wadding and backing to ⅛ inch / 3 mm. Sew the eight binding strips into a continuous length. Complete the quilt using the separate binding method to give a finished binding width of ⅜ inch / 1 cm.

This popular 19th century pattern uses two of the most basic building blocks of patchwork – squares and triangles. Suggestive of the formation of migratory birds, the pattern is created by sewing together chains of triangles. The pieced block offers you a chance to perfect your precision piecing. The quick method used in this project makes it a joy to construct.

FLYING GEESE
Skill level: Intermediate

Finished quilt: 29 × 38 inches / 73.7 × 96.5 cm
Finished block: 6³/₈ × 6³/₈ inches / 16.2 × 16.2 cm
Number of blocks: 12

MATERIALS

- ❖ Broken red for background 1 yard / 1 metre
- ❖ Cream 1 yard / 1 metre
- ❖ Assorted red prints for sawtooth border six scraps, 6 × 6 inches / 15.2 × 15.2 cm
- ❖ Contrast prints 12 scraps, 12 × 12 inches / 30.5 × 30.5 cm
- ❖ Backing 31 × 40 inches / 78.7 × 101.6 cm
- ❖ Wadding 31 × 40 inches / 78.7 × 101.6 cm

CUTTING INSTRUCTIONS

✂ Templates are provided if you prefer to use traditional cutting methods. Seam allowances are included in measurements if using the quick-cutting method.

Broken red fabric
1. Cut four strips, 1¹/₄ × 36 inches / 3.2 × 91.5 cm for the binding. Set aside.

2. For setting the blocks on point, cut six **setting squares** (Template K), 6⁷/₈ × 6⁷/₈ inches / 17.5 × 17.5 cm.

3. Cut five squares, 7¹/₄ × 7¹/₄ inches / 18.4 × 18.4 cm in half diagonally to make ten **side triangles** (Template H).

4. Cut two squares, 5³/₈ × 5³/₈ inches / 13.7 × 13.7 cm in half diagonally to make four **corner triangles** (Template J).

5. Cut six squares, 2⁵/₈ × 2⁵/₈ inches / 6.7 × 6.7 cm (Template G) as illustrated. Label and set aside for the sawtooth border.

Cream fabric
1. Cut eleven strips, 1¹/₄ inches / 3.2 cm wide into 288 **E squares**, 1¹/₄ × 1¹/₄ inches / 3.2 × 3.2 cm.

2. Cut two strips, 1⅝ inches/4.1cm wide into 48 squares, 1⅝ × 1⅝ inches/4.1 × 4.1 cm. Cut each square in half diagonally to make 96 **D triangles** (Template D).

3. Cut 30 squares, 2⅝ × 2⅝ inches/6.7 × 6.7 cm (Template G). Label and set aside for the sawtooth border.

Assorted red prints
1. Cut four squares, 2⅝ × 2⅝ inches/6.7 × 6.7 cm (Template G) from **each** of the assorted red prints. You will need 24 squares in all. Set aside for the sawtooth border.

From each of the 12 contrast prints
1. Cut one square, 2 × 2 inches/5.1 × 5.1 cm (Template A).

2. Cut two squares, 3⅞ × 3⅞ inches/9.8 × 9.8 cm (Template B). Cut in half diagonally to make four **B triangles**.

3. Cut four squares, 1⅝ × 1⅝ inches/4.1 × 4.1 cm (Template C).

4. Cut two strips, 2 × 8 inches/5.1 × 20.3 cm. From each strip, cut six rectangles, 1¼ × 2 inches/3.2 × 5.1cm (Template F). These will be used with the **E squares** to quick-piece the flying geese units.

PIECING THE BLOCKS

✂ Each block requires: one **A square**, four **B triangles**, four **C squares**, eight **D triangles**, 24 **E squares**, and 12 **F rectangles**.

1. To quick-piece the flying geese units, refer to the step-by-step instructions which accompany the Evening Star project on page 29. Piece a total of 12 flying geese units for **each** of the contrast fabrics.

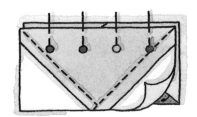

2. Join three flying geese units to make four strips in all.

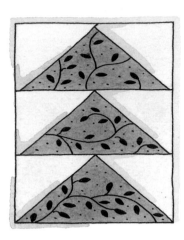

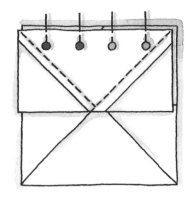

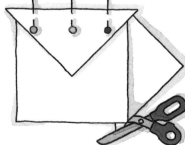

3. Sew a **D triangle** to one side of a **C square**. Press open and trim away the excess points. Sew another **D triangle** to the adjacent side of the square. Press towards the triangle, and trim points. Repeat this sequence until you have pieced four corner units.

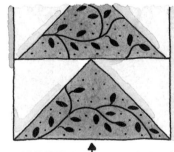

4. Sew a corner unit to each of the four prepared flying geese strips.

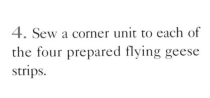

34

5. Sew two **B triangles** to each long side of two flying geese strips.

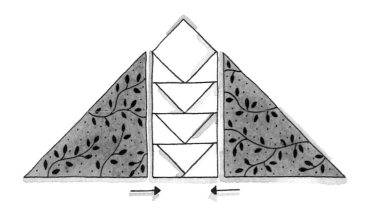

6. Join the remaining two strips to the **central A square**.

2. With right sides together, pin one red print square to one plain square as illustrated. Stitch from one red dot to the next around the sides of the square, pivoting the machine needle at each corner to change directions. Do not stitch into the seam allowance.

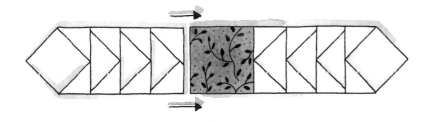

7. Sew all three pieced components together to form the flying geese block.

8. Follow the same sequence to make up the other 11 pieced blocks.

PIECING THE SAWTOOTH BORDER

1. Using the squares set aside for the border, lightly rule intersecting diagonal lines on the plain squares. Next, mark a scant $^1/_4$ inch / 6 mm seam allowance in each corner with a red pencil.

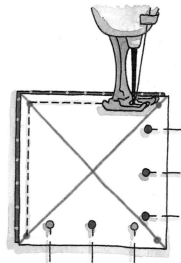

3. Cut across each of the diagonals. Press the triangles open to give four bi-coloured squares, $1^1/_2 \times 1^1/_2$ inches / 3.8×3.8 cm.

4. Mark and sew the rest of the cream and red print squares to make 30 squares in all. Cut on the diagonals to make 120 squares, $1^1/_2 \times 1^1/_2$ inches / 3.8×3.8 cm.

5. Sew the squares together to make two lengths of 24 blocks each and two lengths of 35 blocks each.

PUTTING THE BLOCKS TOGETHER

1. Arrange the blocks and label them 1–12, so that you can keep the blocks in order.

2. Sew two **side triangles** (H) to opposite sides of the **Block 1**.

3. Sew the second diagonal row by alternating a broken red **setting square** (K) between each pieced block.

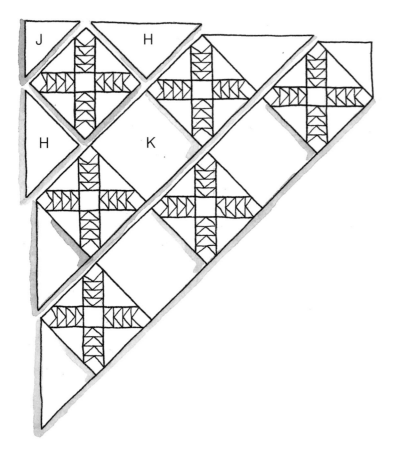

4. Complete the row by sewing a **side triangle** (H) to each end. Press.

5. Sew the four remaining diagonal rows pressing seam allowances towards the darker fabric.

6. Sew the rows together in the correct order and complete the pieced top by sewing on the four **corner triangles** (J).

ADDING THE BORDERS

1. Carefully press the quilt top. Top and bottom measurements should be the same. Each side should be equal as well.

2. Pin a 24 block border to the sides of the quilt. It may be necessary to adjust the length of the border by sewing larger or smaller seam allowances between the sawtooth blocks. Spread the adjustment over several units.

3. Sew the remaining border lengths to the top and bottom, adjusting to fit as before.

QUILTING & FINISHING

1. Press the quilt top carefully taking care not to stretch or distort the piecing. Trim away loose threads and tidy up the back.

2. Using the quilting templates supplied, transfer the quilting patterns to the **setting squares**, **side** and **corner triangles**. The pieced blocks will be outline quilted, and do not require marking.

3. Assemble the backing, wadding and pieced top. Pin, then baste thoroughly in a grid no more than 2 inches / 5.1 cm apart.

4. Use gold or red thread to quilt the **setting squares**, **side** and **corner triangles**.

5. Match the quilting thread to each flying geese block and quilt according to the quilting plan.

6. Trim the backing and wadding even with the edges of the quilt top.

7. Sew the binding strips together into a continuous length.

8. Finish the raw edges using the separate binding method described in the Techniques section.

BOW-TIE

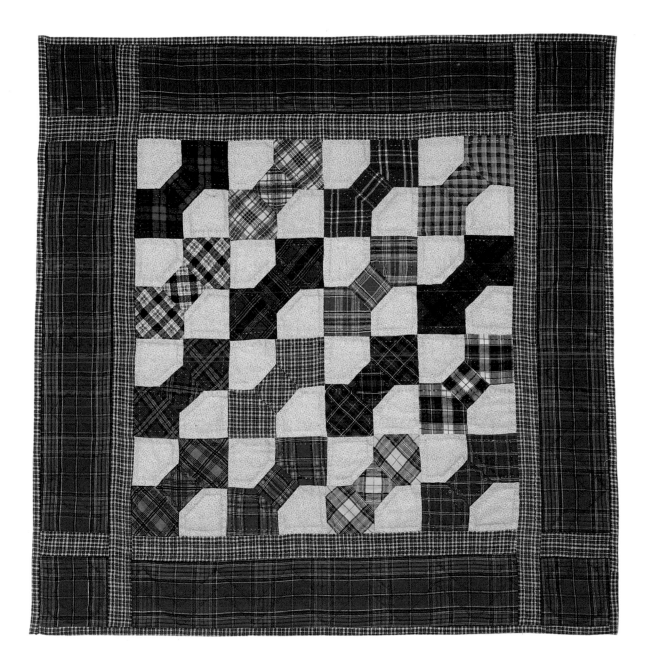

Bow-tie is one of those universally appealing patterns that beguiles even the most skilled needlewomen. In this version, the plaids and checks recall the days when the jauntiest 'best beaus' came to call wearing straw hats and bow-ties. Change the direction of the Bow-tie blocks to the Snowball Set and you have a lovely clear space to show off your best quilting. For another interpretation, use this pattern to showcase a fabric collection from the '30s. For an evocative memory quilt, make blocks from all your favourite dresses or your husband's cherished, but worn ties.

BOW-TIE

Skill level: Intermediate

Finished quilt: 24 × 24 inches / 61 × 61 cm
Finished block: 4 × 4 inches / 10.2 × 10.2 cm
Number of blocks: 16

MATERIALS

❖ Plaids and checks for Bow-ties 16 different scraps, each 7 × 8 inches / 17.8 × 20.3 cm
❖ Yellow for background ¼ yard / 25 cm
❖ Green check for inner border and binding ¼ yard / 25 cm
❖ Red plaid for outer border ¼ yard / 25 cm
❖ Backing 26 × 26 inches / 66 × 66 cm
❖ Wadding 26 × 26 inches / 66 × 66 cm

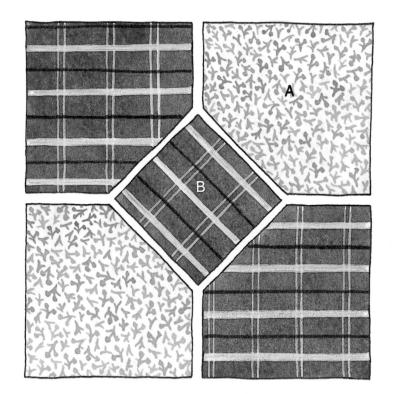

CUTTING INSTRUCTIONS

✂ Make **Templates A** and **B** following the instructions in the Techniques section. Trace around each template on the wrong side of the fabric with a sharp pencil. Transfer the red dots to indicate corner seam allowances. The pencil line is your sewing line. Add a scant ¼ inch / 6 mm seam allowance by eye as you cut out each piece.

Yellow fabric
1. Cut 32 pieces using **Template A**. You will need two for the background of each Bow-tie block.

Green check fabric
1. For the inner border, cut four strips 1½ × 16½ inches / 3.8 × 41.9 cm, two strips 1½ × 24½ inches / 3.8 × 62.2 cm, and four strips 1½ × 3½ inches / 3.8 × 8.9 cm.

2. For the binding, cut three strips, 1¼ inch / 3.2 cm wide across the full width of the fabric.

Plaid and check fabrics
1. From each scrap, cut two pieces using **Template A** and one piece using **Template B**.

Red plaid
1. For the outer border, cut four strips 3½ × 16½ inches / 8.9 × 41.9 cm. Next, cut four corner squares, 3½ × 3½ inches / 8.9 × 8.9 cm.

PIECING THE BLOCKS

 Refer to specific instructions on hand-piecing in the Techniques section.

1. Sew the plaid Bow-tie first, by joining the **A pieces** to opposite sides of a **B square**.

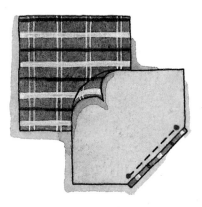

Starting with a double back-stitch, sew exactly along the pencil line between the two red dots as indicated.

2. Now sew the **background A pieces** to the other two sides of the plaid **B square**, one at a time. As before, stitch on the pencil line, without extending into the seam allowance.

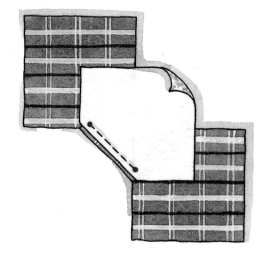

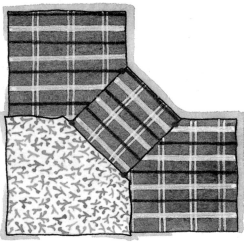

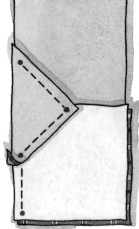

3. Sew the two remaining sides of each **background A piece** to the plaid Bow-tie as illustrated.

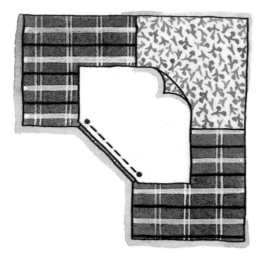

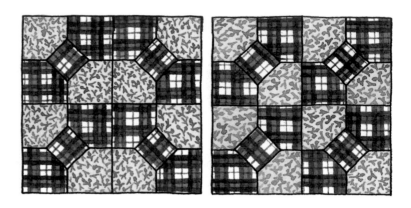

2. Keeping the blocks in order, pin, then sew four blocks together to form the first row. Sew three more rows. Finally, sew the rows together to form the pieced top.

4. Repeat this sequence until you have sewn all 16 Bow-tie blocks.

ADDING THE BORDERS

1. Join the 16$\frac{1}{2}$ inch / 41.9 cm red plaid and green check border strips together. Press towards the darker fabric.

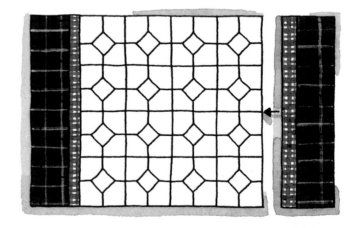

PUTTING THE BLOCKS TOGETHER

1. Lay out the 16 blocks in a pleasing arrangement. Changing the orientation of the blocks will give you several alternative designs. Keep in mind that the perimeter blocks will need to complement the green check of the inner border.

2. Sew these pieced border strips to opposite sides of the quilt top and press again.

3. Sew a 24$\frac{1}{2}$ inch / 62.2 cm green border strip to the top and bottom. Press.

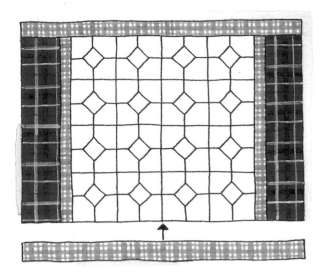

3. Assemble the backing, wadding and quilt top. Pin and baste securely.

4. Outline quilt ¼ inch / 6 mm from all seams on each Bow-tie block. Quilt the borders and corner blocks as marked. Quilt in-the-ditch on both seams of the narrow green border.

5. Trim away excess wadding and backing even with the raw edges of the quilt top.

6. Join the 1¼ inch / 3.2 cm binding strips to make a continuous length of binding, and finish the raw edges of the quilt using the separate binding method described in the Techniques section.

4. Make up the corner units by first sewing a short green check border strip to each of the four corner squares.

5. Sew a 16½ inch / 41.9 cm red plaid border strip between two corner units. Press towards the green fabric.

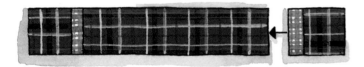

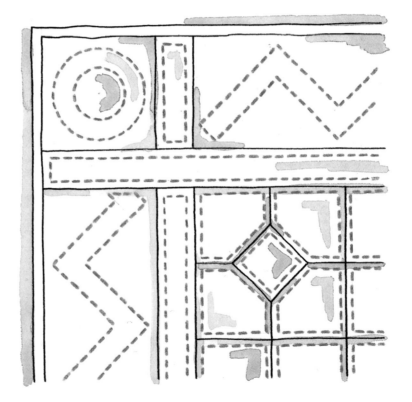

6. Finally, sew the pieced border to the top and bottom of the quilt. Press towards the green sashing.

QUILTING & FINISHING

1. Press the quilt top carefully.

2. Transfer the quilting patterns to the red plaid borders and corner squares.

Appliqué Quilts

Pennsylvania Wreath

Flowerpots

Tulips

Bluebird

The inspiration for this small quilt is a larger version made in the 1920s. The original, now in a private collection, is testimony that faded and worn heirloom quilts can often be more beautiful now than when first made. Once a vibrant palette of pink, burgundy, blue and green, today only the indigo blues, claret reds and acid greens remain to remind us of its vivid beginnings. Modern antique look-alike fabrics make it possible to reproduce the quilt's softly, faded charm. As your appliqué project will involve using very small pieces, select only the best quality, finely woven fabrics. If for any reason you want to use a coarser fabric that frays easily, stabilise first by ironing it to a fusible interfacing, cut to the exact shape of the template.

PENNSYLVANIA WREATH

Skill level: Confident intermediate

Finished quilt: $22^{1}/_{4} \times 22^{1}/_{4}$ inches / 56.5×56.5 cm
Finished block: $8^{1}/_{4} \times 8^{1}/_{4}$ inches / 21×21 cm
Number of blocks: 4

MATERIALS

- ❖ Cream for background $^{1}/_{3}$ yard / 30 cm
- ❖ Small-scale print scraps – a variety of scraps in beige, cream, brown, pink, dark red, indigo blue, soft grey and acid green. Tiny pieces are acceptable, as each leaf requires a scrap no larger than $1^{1}/_{4} \times 2$ inches / 3.2×5.1 cm, and each heart, a piece $2^{1}/_{2} \times 2^{1}/_{4}$ inches / 6.4×5.7 cm.
- ❖ Soft grey for inner border $^{1}/_{8}$ yard / 15 cm
- ❖ Dusty rose for outer border $^{1}/_{3}$ yard / 30 cm
- ❖ Dark rose for binding $^{1}/_{4}$ yard / 25 cm
- ❖ Light weight interfacing (optional) $^{1}/_{3}$ yard / 30 cm
- ❖ Backing 26×26 inches / 66×66 cm
- ❖ Wadding 26×26 inches / 66×66 cm
- ❖ 2 skeins of 6-strand embroidery thread OR $2^{1}/_{2}$ yards / 2 metres very fine soutache braid OR machine embroider using a narrow satin stitch

CUTTING INSTRUCTIONS

1. From the cream fabric, cut one strip, 11 inches / 27.9 cm wide across the full width. Cut this strip down into four squares, 11 × 11 inches / 27.9 × 27.9 cm. Although the finished block is 8¼ inches / 21 cm, you will find it easier to work with a larger foundation square when applying small shapes.

2. Use **Template A** to trace at least 116 leaves from your small-scale prints. Add ¼ inch / 6 mm seam allowance as you cut. Cut 12 to 24 more leaves than you actually need as it is important to have a large selection to achieve a good colour balance.

3. Use **Template B** to trace 32 hearts from the darker colours for the corner and centre hearts. Remember to add ¼ inch / 6 mm seam allowance as you cut.

3a. If using interfacing, trace and cut the required number of leaves and hearts, but do not add seam allowances.

4. If using soutache braid for the wreath circle, cut four pieces, 20 inches / 50.8 cm long.

5. For the inner border, cut four strips, 1⅛ × 30 inches / 2.9 × 76.2 cm.

6. For the outer border, cut four strips, 2¾ × 30 inches / 7 × 76.2 cm.

7. For the binding, cut three strips, 1½ × 44 inches / 3.8 × 111.8 cm.

SEWING THE BLOCKS

1. To find the centre of the background block, fold it in half, across both diagonals. Press lightly to define the fold lines only. Fold vertically and horizontally and press again.

2. Place a compass point at the centre of the square and draw a circle with a radius of 2⅞ inches / 7.3 cm.

3. Mark two concentric squares, one 8¼ inches / 21 cm and the other 8¾ inches / 22.2 cm around the centre of each foundation block. The smaller square is the finished size of the block; the larger is the trim size after completing the appliqué.

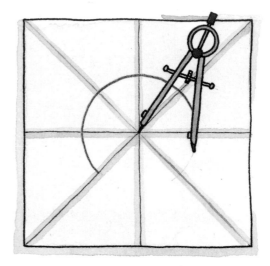

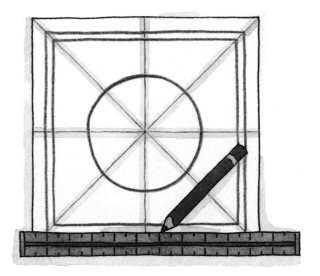

4. Separate all the strands in a 25 inch / 63.5 cm length of embroidery cotton. Embroider all four circles with chain stitch using only five strands. If you prefer to use soutache braid, turn under ¼ inch / 6 mm at one end and pin all around the circle. Use matching thread and sew the braid with a simple running stitch to the pencil line. Complete the circle by turning under ¼ inch / 6 mm and butting the ends.

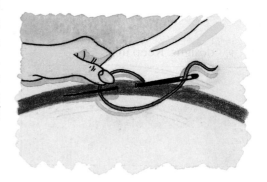

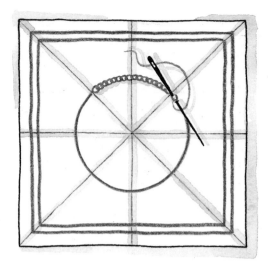

5. Choose 29 leaves to make the first wreath. Arrange 18 around the outside of the circle following the block plan. Pin, baste and appliqué in place. For detailed information of how to make sharp points when appliquing small shapes, refer to the Techniques section.

6. Pin and baste 11 leaves around the inside of the circle. Appliqué in place.

7. Use the horizontal and vertical fold lines to position the four hearts in the centre of the wreath. Pin, baste and appliqué in place.

8. Use the diagonal fold lines to position the corner hearts. Pin, baste and appliqué the hearts to complete the block. Now appliqué the other three blocks.

47

9. Cut each appliqué block down to 8 3/4 inches / 22.2 cm. Sew the four blocks together and press.

ADDING THE BORDERS

1. Sew the inner (grey) and outer (rose) border strips together. Treat them as a single border unit from now on. Make three more pieced borders with the remaining grey and rose strips.

2. Refer to the instructions for adding borders and mitring in the Techniques section.

QUILTING & FINISHING

1. Press the quilt top thoroughly, without flattening the appliqué.

2. Following the quilt plan, mark the quilting pattern on the borders using a ruler and sharp marking pencil.

3. Assemble the quilt layers – backing, wadding and quilt top. Pin and baste all three layers securely. Baste 1/4 inch / 6 mm all around the outside edge of the quilt to stabilise it until it is bound.

4. Outline quilt 1/8 inch / 3 mm from the seam allowances between the appliqué blocks, from the edges of the leaves and from the edges of the hearts.

5. Quilt in-the-ditch on both sides of the inner border. Quilt diagonal parallel lines on the wide outer border, as marked.

6. Trim the backing and wadding 1/8 inch / 3 mm larger than the quilt top.

7. Sew the binding strips together into a continuous length and bind following the instructions for separate binding in the Techniques section.

8. Quilt in-the-ditch along the inside edge of the binding, and remove all basting stitches to finish.

FLOWERPOTS

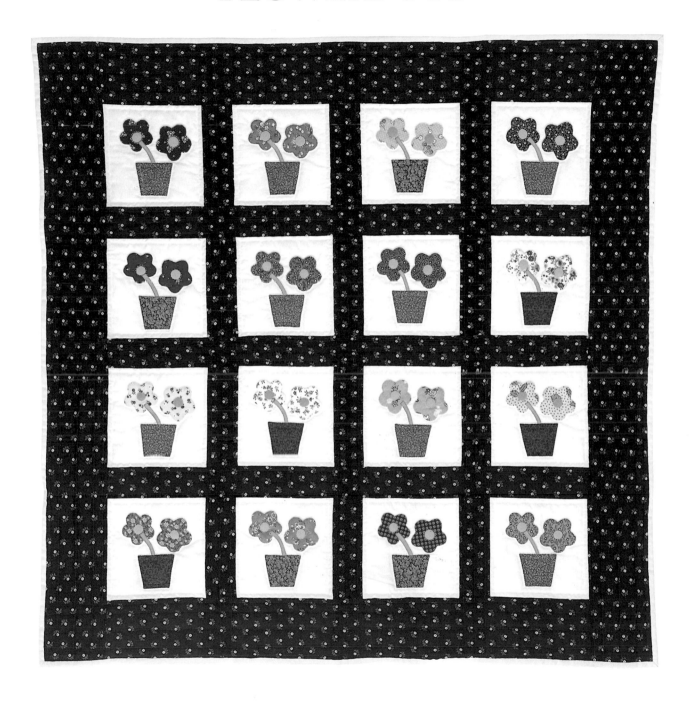

No windowsill full of plants was ever more orderly than these cheerful, perpetually blooming pots. They are proof that the simplest flower shapes can provide endless pleasure. In this instance, a biscuit cutter decided the shape of the flower. Inspired by a 1930s quilt, now in the Museum Quilts collection in London, this small wallhanging takes its particular charm from a rich assortment of period fabrics and the novel treatment of the stems.

FLOWERPOTS

Skill level: Intermediate

Finished quilt: 36×36 inches / 91.4×91.4 cm
Finished block: $5^1/_2 \times 5^1/_2$ inches / 14×14 cm
Number of blocks: 16

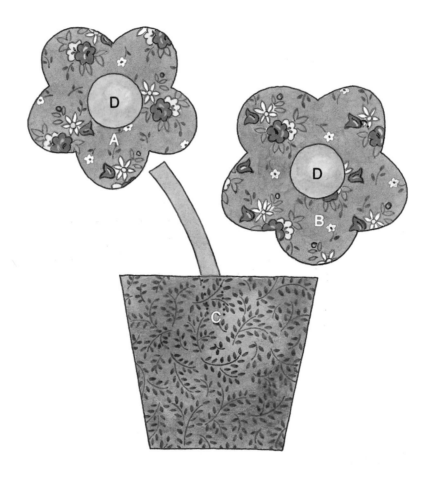

MATERIALS

❖ Cream $^5/_8$ yard / 60 cm
❖ Dark blue print 1 yard / 1 metre
❖ 16 scraps of small-scale floral prints for flowers, each at least 3×5 inches / 7.6×12.7 cm
❖ 16 scraps of dark green prints for flowerpots, each at least 3×4 inches / 7.6×10.2 cm

❖ Scrap of yellow for flower centres, at least 8×8 inches / 20.3×20.3 cm
❖ Green bias binding 1 yard / 1 metre
❖ Small scraps medium-weight, iron-on interfacing
❖ Backing/binding 40×40 inches / 101.6×101.6 cm
❖ Wadding 38×38 inches / 96.5×96.5 cm

CUTTING INSTRUCTIONS

✂ Remember, when using templates, the pencil line is your sewing line. Add a scant ¹/₄ inch / 6 mm seam allowance as you cut each piece.

Cream background fabric
1. Cut 16 squares, 6 × 6 inches / 15.2 × 15.2 cm.

Blue print
1. For the borders, cut two strips, 4¹/₂ × 36 inches / 11.4 × 91.4 cm and two strips, 4¹/₂ × 28 inches / 11.4 × 71.2 cm.
2. For the sashing, cut three strips, 2¹/₂ × 28 inches / 6.4 × 71.2 cm and 12 strips, 2¹/₂ × 6 inches / 6.4 × 15.2 cm.

Floral prints
1. Cut one flower **A** and one flower **B** from each scrap.

Dark green scraps
1. Using **Template C**, cut 16 flowerpots.

Iron-on interfacing
1. Using **Template D**, cut 32 circles. Do not add seam allowance as you cut.

Yellow scraps
1. Using **Template D**, cut 32 circles.

Green bias binding
1. Cut 16 lengths, each 2 inches / 5.1 cm long.

SEWING THE BLOCKS

1. Arrange Flowers **A** and **B** on a background block. Refer to the diagram, or use a template as a placement guide. First baste, then appliqué the flowers in place.

2. Prepare green stems by folding the bias binding in half lengthwise. Turn  under one end and trim on the wrong side to reduce bulk.

3. Pin and baste in place. Stitch down using a tiny blindstitch. The raw end of the stem will be hidden under the flowerpot.

4. Turn under and baste the seam allowances of the flowerpots. Trim excess seam allowance to ¹/₈ inch / 3 mm.

5. Baste the flowerpots to the background block, then appliqué in place, taking care to cover the raw end of the stem.

6. Following the manufacturer's instructions, iron interfacing circles to the wrong side of the large yellow flower centres.

7. Using a fine needle, sew around the outside of each flower centre with very small gathering stitches. Leave enough thread at the beginning and end to tie.

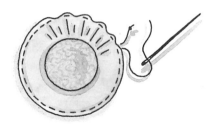

8. Tie the ends together and pull gently, gathering the excess fabric around the interfacing until you have formed a perfect circle. Do not trim away any of the fabric on the wrong side. The gathered seam allowance will slightly pad each flower centre giving it a raised effect. Appliqué each centre in place as illustrated.

9. Make another 15 blocks following the same sequence.

PUTTING THE BLOCKS TOGETHER

1. Lay out the 16 flowerpot blocks in a pleasing arrangement. Keeping the blocks in order, make up four horizontal rows of four blocks each. Alternate a short sashing strip between each appliqué block as illustrated. Press all seam allowances towards the blue sashing.

2. Sew four rows of flowerpots to three long sashing strips. Press seam allowances towards the long blue sashes.

3. Sew the short borders to the top and bottom of the quilt, then add the longer side borders. Press the seam allowances towards the borders.

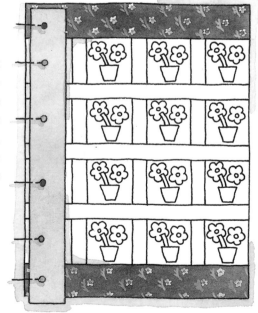

QUILTING & FINISHING

1. Press the pieced top carefully. This is the final pressing before quilting.

2. Mark the border and sashing with a simple quilting design of your choice.

3. Assemble the quilt layers together, baste and outline quilt around the flowers, flower centres and flowerpots. Quilt the border and sashing as marked.

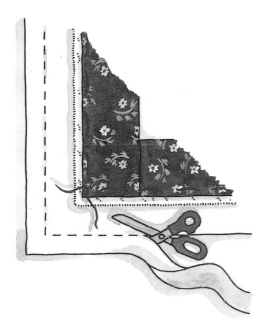

4. Bind the raw edges of the quilt by using the self-binding method. Trim the wadding even with the quilt top and trim the backing to leave a ⅝ inch / 1.5 cm border all around.

5. Turn under and press a ¼ inch / 6 mm seam allowance along the four edges of the backing. Bring the backing to the front and slipstitch the folded edge.

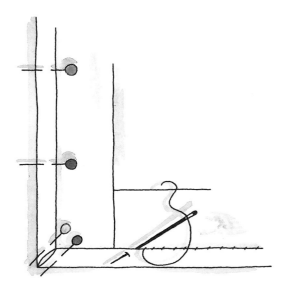

6. Finally, quilt in-the-ditch along the edge of the binding to give added definition.

Appliqué quilts reached a peak of popularity during the first half of the 20th century. Syndicated newspaper columns reached needlewomen across the country with an enormous variety of appliqué patterns. None were more popular than flowers, and they appeared in all styles and degrees of sophistication. The 'municipal' green, a hallmark of public buildings in the '20s and '30s became part of the quilter's palette of the period and provides a wonderful counterpoint for the bright colours of the tulips.

TULIPS

Skill level: Beginner

Finished quilt: $19^1/4 \times 19^1/4$ inches / 48.9×48.9 cm
Finished block: $4^1/2 \times 4^1/2$ inches / 11.4×11.4 cm
Number of blocks: 13

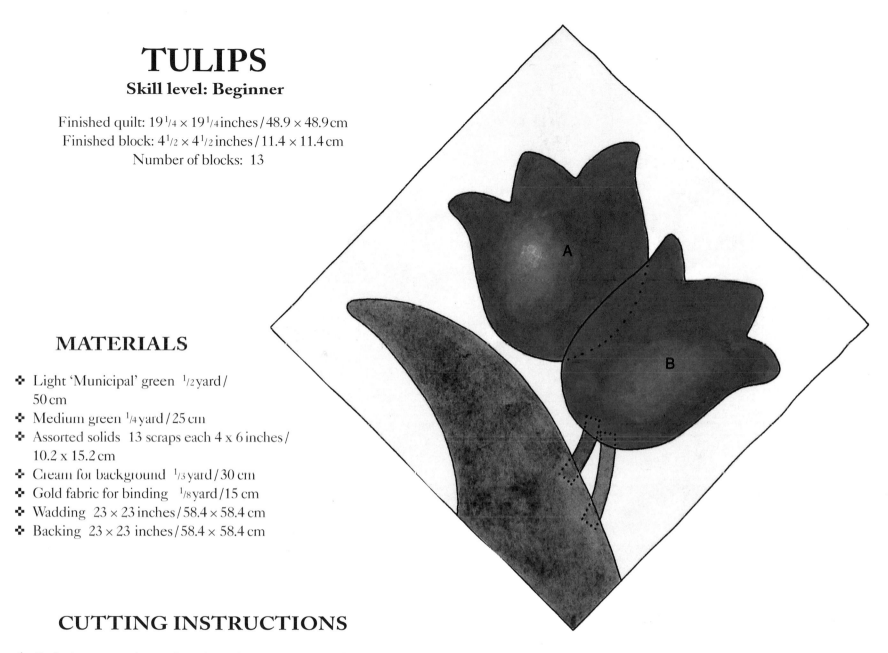

MATERIALS

❖ Light 'Municipal' green $^1/2$ yard /
   50 cm
❖ Medium green $^1/4$ yard / 25 cm
❖ Assorted solids 13 scraps each 4 x 6 inches /
   10.2 x 15.2 cm
❖ Cream for background $^1/3$ yard / 30 cm
❖ Gold fabric for binding $^1/8$ yard / 15 cm
❖ Wadding 23×23 inches / 58.4×58.4 cm
❖ Backing 23×23 inches / 58.4×58.4 cm

CUTTING INSTRUCTIONS

1. Referring to your layout for colour placement, trace and cut one **Tulip A** and one **Tulip B** from each of the nine solid scraps, with templates right side up. Cut the tulips for the remaining four blocks with the templates face down, to give you the **'reverse'** tulips for **Rows 2** and **4**.

2. Place the leaf template right side up on the right side of the medium green fabric, trace and cut nine leaves. Trace and cut four more leaves with the template face down, to give you the **'reverse'** leaves for **Rows 2** and **4**.

3. For the stems, cut four bias strips $^1/2 \times 9$ inches / 1.3×22.9 cm.

4. From the gold fabric, cut two strips $1^1/4$ inches / 3.2 cm wide across the full width of the material for the binding.

5. Cut 13 **background squares**, 5×5 inches / 12.7×12.7 cm from the cream fabric (Template C).

6. From the light green fabric, cut four squares, $5^3/8 \times 5^3/8$ inches / 13.7×13.7 cm. Cut in half diagonally to make eight **side triangles** (Template D).

7. Cut two squares 4×4 inches / 10.2×10.2 cm. Cut in half diagonally to make four **corner triangles** (Template E).

55

SEWING THE BLOCKS

✂ Because the tulips have some acute angles, it is easier to appliqué using the needle-turning method. Refer to the Techniques section for detailed directions.

1. To prepare the blocks for appliqué, place the cream background squares over a photocopy of the exploded diagram and lightly trace placement lines onto nine blocks with a sharp marking pencil. To make it easier to see the outline of the design, you may need to darken the lines on the photocopy. **For the four blocks in horizontal Rows 2 and 4, placement lines will be reversed so you will trace the mirror image**.

2. To make the stems, fold and press the bias binding. Trim the raw edge so that it does not show on the right side. Cut the prepared bias strips into 13 lengths, $1\frac{1}{4}$ inches / 3.2 cm for the long stems, and 13 lengths, $\frac{3}{4}$ inch / 1.9 cm for the short stems.

3. Pin all 26 stems in position on the background squares, then appliqué ensuring that the ends will be hidden by the leaf and tulips.

4. Pin a leaf shape in place, making sure that the base fits into the bottom of the background square. Baste and appliqué the leaf.

5. Pin, baste and appliqué **Tulip A**. Pin and baste **Tulip B** so that it overlaps **Tulip A** on the dotted line. Appliqué **Tulip B** to complete the block.

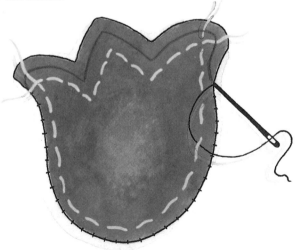

6. Appliqué 13 blocks in all. Nine will incline to the left, and four to the right.

7. Lightly press each block on the wrong side so the appliqué shapes do not flatten.

PUTTING THE BLOCKS TOGETHER

1. On a flat surface, arrange the blocks according to your colour plan.

2. Sew a **side D triangle** to opposite sides of a **Tulip block**. Press seam allowances towards the green fabric.

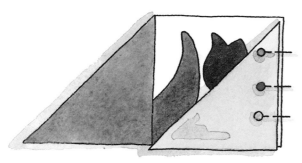

3. Sew the next four diagonal rows together in order, adding side triangles at each end. Press seam allowances between the appliqué blocks open.

4. Sew the five diagonal rows together. Press seam allowances open.

5. Sew an **E triangle** to each corner to complete the quilt top. Press seam allowances towards the green fabric.

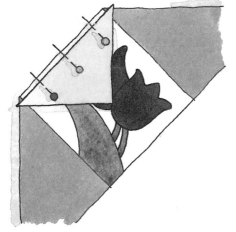

6. Press the quilt top carefully, taking care not to stretch the blocks or flatten the appliqué by pressing too hard.

QUILTING & FINISHING

1. Mark leaf veins and tulip quilting lines with a sharp marking pencil.

2. Tape the backing right side down to a flat surface. Centre the wadding and quilt top on the backing and smooth out the layers. Pin and baste securely.

3. Quilt the tulips and leaves with matching thread.

4. Outline quilt ⅛ inch / 3 mm around each leaf, tulip and stem with cream quilting thread.

5. Quilt a scant ¼ inch / 6 mm from the seam allowance of each appliqué block, then echo quilt parallel lines ¼ inch / 6 mm and ¾ inch / 1.9 cm from the seam allowance on each green side and corner triangle.

6. Trim the backing and wadding to within ¼ inch / 6 mm of the edge of the quilt top.

7. To round the corners, trace around a large spool of thread and trim the backing and wadding away at each corner.

8. Sew the gold binding strips together into a continuous length. Follow the instructions for separate binding in the Techniques section.

This delightful bird is representative of the folk art tradition popular in mid-19th century quilts. As Americans moved westwards, women often made quilts to record pictures of the world around them. These quilts contained houses, birds, farm scenes and images of everyday life. The simplicity of the original 1920s quilt which inspired this project, lends itself perfectly to being scaled down. The 5 inch/12.7cm block has small pieces, but is not too difficult to handle.

BLUEBIRD

Skill level: Confident beginner

Finished quilt: 26 × 26 inches / 66 × 66 cm
Finished block: 5 × 5 inches / 12.7 × 12.7 cm
Number of blocks: 9

MATERIALS

- Cream fabric ¹/₂ yard / 50 cm
- Red fabric ¹/₂ yard / 50 cm
- Blue fabric ¹/₄ yard / 25 cm
- Green fabric ¹/₈ yard / 15 cm
- Brown fabric ¹/₈ yard / 15 cm

- Red check ¹/₈ yard / 15 cm
- Wadding 28 × 28 inches / 71.1 × 71.1 cm
- Backing 28 × 28 inches / 71.1 × 71.1 cm
- One skein gold pearl cotton for the beak, eye and legs

CUTTING INSTRUCTIONS

✂ Templates for appliqué do not include seam allowances. With a hard pencil, trace around the template, right side up, on the right side of the fabric. This will be your sewing line. As you cut out each piece, add a ¼ inch / 6 mm seam allowance for turning under raw edges.

Brown fabric
1. Using **Template A**, cut nine branches from the brown fabric.

Green fabric
1. Using **Template B**, cut 27 green leaves. Make sure to mark each leaf with a '**B**', so you do not confuse them with the '**C**' leaves.

2. Cut 18 green leaves using **Template C**.

Blue fabric
1. Cut three strips, 1¼ inches / 3.2 cm across the full width of the fabric. From one strip cut two lengths of 21½ inches / 54.6 cm. From the remaining strips cut two lengths of 23 inches / 58.4 cm. Set these strips aside for the inner border.

2. Cut nine bodies using **Template D**.

Red fabric
1. Cut nine breasts using **Template E**.

2. Cut 24 sashing strips, 2 × 5½ inches / 5.1 × 14 cm.

Cream fabric
1. Cut nine background squares, 5½ × 5½ inches / 14 × 14 cm.

Red check
1. For the outer border, cut four strips, 2 inches / 5.1 cm wide across the full width of the fabric. Cut each strip down to 30 inches / 76.2 cm. Extra length has been allowed for mitring the corners.

2. Cut the leftover border strips into 16 squares, 2 × 2 inches / 5.1 × 5.1 cm, for the posts.

SEWING THE BLOCKS

✂ In preparation for appliqué, turn under and baste the seam allowances of the **branches**, **leaves** and **bodies**. Do not turn under the base of the leaves as these will be tucked under the branches.

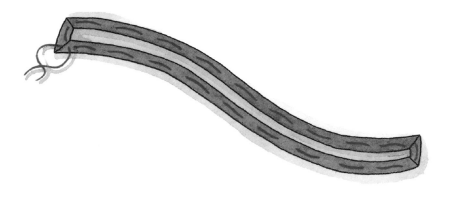

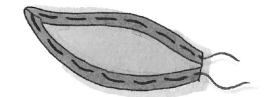

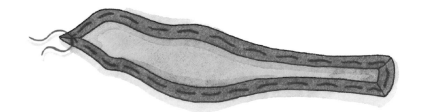

For placement guidelines, either photocopy or trace the block from the book, then darken all lines with a permanent pen. Trace the design onto the cream fabric with a hard lead pencil.

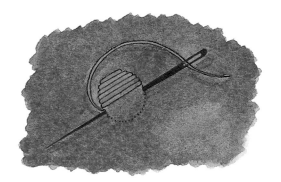

1. Position the prepared branch onto the background block according to your traced placement lines. Baste in place down the centre of each branch.

2. Place the **B** and **C** leaves on either side, and at the top of the branch. Tuck the base of each leaf under the branch and baste in place. Use matching thread to slipstitch the leaves and branches to the background block.

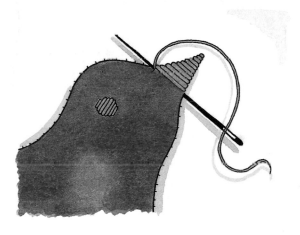

3. Prepare all nine blocks to this stage.

4. Slipstitch the basted edge of the **bird's body D**, to the pencil sewing line of the **red breast, E**. This step can be done by machine, if you prefer.

5. Place the bird across the branch to follow the traced pattern, and baste roughly in place. Slipstitch to the background using matching thread as before.

6. Thread an embroidery needle with a single strand of gold pearl cotton embroidery floss. Embroider the bird's eye, beak and legs in satin stitch as shown.

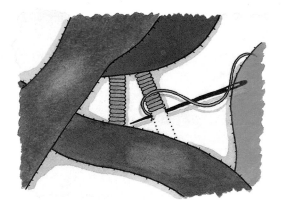

7. Complete the remaining eight blocks.

PUTTING THE BLOCKS TOGETHER

1. Arrange the bluebird blocks into three rows. Pin, then sew red sashing strips to separate each block, and to begin and end each row. Four sashing strips will be used in each horizontal row. Press seams towards the sashing strips.

2. Sew the four horizontal sashing strips by alternating red check posts with solid red sashing strips. Press seams towards the sashing strips.

3. Join the bluebird rows to the rows of posts and sashing to make up the quilt top. Press seams towards the bluebird rows.

ADDING THE BORDERS

1. Pin, then sew the blue inner border strips to the sides of the quilt. Press seams out to the border before adding on the top and bottom border strips. Press again.

2. Pin, then sew the red check outer border strips to the quilt. Follow the instructions for mitred borders described in the Techniques section.

QUILTING & FINISHING

1. Press the quilt top carefully, trimming away all loose threads that may show through the cream fabric.

2. From the quilting pattern below transfer the small heart (A) to each post, and the larger heart (B) to each block.

3. Assemble the quilt layers and baste. Outline quilt the bird, leaves, branches and sashing. Quilt in-the-ditch around each block. Remove basting stitches.

4. Finish the raw edges of the quilt using the fold-finish method described in the Techniques section.

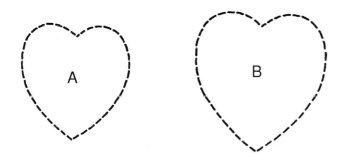

Amish & Mennonite Quilts

Basket of Chips

Double Irish Chain

Trip Around the World

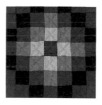

Courthouse Steps

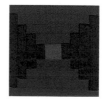

Nine-patch

Pieced in elect ic blue and contrasting green, this distinctly modern design is actually based on a 1920s Pennsylvania Amish quilt. Although deceptively simple-looking, this miniature requires the most careful measuring and precision piecing, and the modern quilter would do well to heed the old carpenter's adage 'measure twice, cut once'. The half-square piecing technique ensures greater accuracy when working with small triangles, and will help achieve the sharp points of the baskets and chips, necessary to give the design its crisp definition.

BASKET OF CHIPS

Skill level: Intermediate

Finished quilt: 30 × 35¹/₂ inches / 76.2 × 90.2 cm
Finished block: 4 × 4 inches / 10.2 × 10.2 cm
Number of blocks: 20 baskets and 12 plain blocks

MATERIALS

- ❖ Royal blue 1¹/₃ yards / 1.25 metres
- ❖ Emerald green 1¹/₄ yards / one metre
- ❖ Wadding 32 × 37¹/₂ inches / 81.3 × 95.3 cm
- ❖ Backing 32 × 37¹/₂ inches / 81.3 × 95.3 cm

CUTTING INSTRUCTIONS

Blue fabric
1. Cut two strips, 2¹/₂ × 36 inches / 6.4 × 91.4 cm and two strips, 2¹/₂ × 40 inches / 6.4 × 101.6 cm for the border.
2. Cut one strip, 1⁷/₈ inches / 4.8 cm wide across the full width of the fabric. Cut the strip down into 20 squares, 1⁷/₈ inch / 4.8 cm. Finally, cut each square in half diagonally to give you 40 **B triangles**; two are needed for the base of each basket.
3. Cut 12 **E squares**, 4¹/₂ × 4¹/₂ inches / 11.4 × 11.4 cm.
4. Cut 14 **F side triangles** and four **G corner triangles**. Be sure to align the arrow of the template on the correct grain.
5. Cut ten squares, 3³/₄ × 3³/₄ inches / 9.5 × 9.5 cm. These will be paired with the green squares of the same size to make the **B–B bi-coloured squares**.
6. Cut three squares, 5³/₄ × 5³/₄ inches / 14.6 × 14.6 cm. These will be paired with the green squares of the same size to make the **C–C bi-coloured squares**.

Green fabric
1. Cut two strips, 1¹/₂ × 27 inches / 3.8 × 9.4 cm and two strips, 1¹/₂ × 33 inches / 3.8 × 9.4 cm for the border.
2. Cut two strips, 2¹/₂ inches / 6.4 cm wide across the full width of the fabric. Cut the strips down into 40 **D rectangles**, 1¹/₂ × 2¹/₂ inches / 3.8 × 6.4 cm.
3. Cut two strips, 2⁷/₈ inches / 7.3 cm wide across the full width of the fabric. Cut the strips down into ten 2⁷/₈ inch / 7.3 × 7.3 cm squares, then in half diagonally to give you 20 **C triangles**.
4. Cut one strip, 1¹/₂ × 36 inches / 3.8 × 91.4 cm. Cut the strip down to give 20 **A squares**.
5. For the binding, cut four strips, 2 inches / 5.1 cm wide across the full width of the fabric.

6. Cut ten squares, 3³/₄ × 3³/₄ inches / 9.5 × 9.5 cm. These will be used to match up with blue **B triangles** to make the **B–B bi-coloured squares**.

7. Cut three squares, 5³/₄ × 5³/₄ inches / 14.6 × 14.6 cm. These will be used to make the **C–C bi-coloured squares**.

HALF-SQUARE QUICK-PIECING TECHNIQUE

Follow this sequence with both the **3³/₄ inch / 9.5 cm** and **5³/₄ inch / 14.6 cm squares**:

1. With right sides together and all edges matching, place a green square on top of a blue square. Rule two intersecting diagonal lines through the top square with a pencil.

2. Using the pencil lines as your sewing guide, sew ¹/₄ inch / 6 mm on either side of each diagonal line. It is critical that you sew an accurate seam allowance.

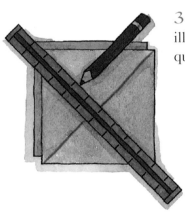

3. Draw two more pencil lines as illustrated to divide the square into quarters.

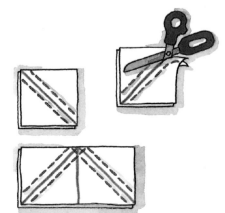

4. Cut along each of the four pencil lines to separate the square into eight half-square units. Press the bi-coloured units open, with the seam allowances towards the blue fabric. Finally, trim down excess seams to ¹/₈ inch / 3 mm.

PIECING THE BLOCKS

1. Sew the **B–B units** together into pairs as illustrated. You will need 20 units with the blue triangle on the right, and 20 with the blue triangle on the left. Press.

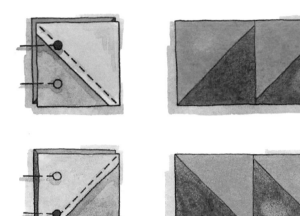

2. Sew an **A square** to the blue edge of a pair of **B–B squares** to make a **BB–BB–A unit**. Press. Make 20 units.

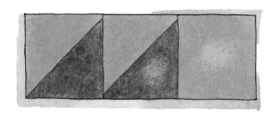

3. Sew the remaining **B–B pairs** to the **C–C squares** until you have made 20 **CC–BB–BB units**. Press.

4. Sew these two units together to form the 'chips'. Press.

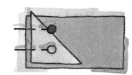

5. Sew a blue **B triangle** to a **D rectangle** to make a **left-hand unit**. Continue until you have 20 units.

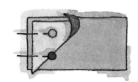

6. Now sew 20 **right-hand B–D units** making sure to reverse the B triangle, as illustrated.

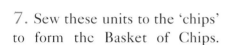

7. Sew these units to the 'chips' to form the Basket of Chips.

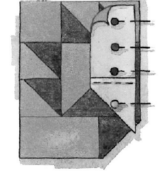

8. Finish the block by sewing a **C triangle** to the diagonal edge, being careful to off-set the points of the triangle. Sew 20 blocks in all.

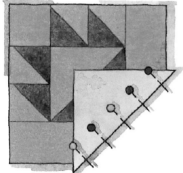

PUTTING THE BLOCKS TOGETHER

1. Join the pieced blocks to the plain blue blocks, finishing each end of a diagonal row with an **F setting triangle**.

2. Sew the diagonal rows together to form the quilt top. Sew the four **G corner triangles** on last.

ADDING THE BORDERS

✂ To make it easier to mitre a double border, sew the border strips of the same length together and treat them as a single unit.

1. Sew the blue and green, 36 inch/91.4 cm border strips together. Press towards the blue fabric. Fold in half, and with a pin mark the mid-point on the green strip.

2. Follow the same sequence with the blue and green, 40 inch/101.6 cm border strips.

3. Use a pin to mark the mid-point of each side of the quilt top.

4. Pin the longer border strips to opposite sides of the quilt, matching mid-points and lining up the raw edge of the green border strip with the raw edge of the quilt. Sew in place, beginning and ending your seam ¼ inch/6 mm from the raw edges. Press the pieced border strips out.

5. Pin, then sew the two remaining borders to the top and bottom of the quilt, matching mid-points as before. **This time, begin and end your stitching at the inner border seam. Do not sew over the border strip.**

6. To finish the corners with a mitre, refer to the instructions in the Techniques section.

QUILTING & FINISHING

1. Press the pieced top thoroughly and carefully. This is the final pressing before the top is quilted.

2. Transfer the quilting pattern to the blue blocks and setting triangles following the quilting diagram. Working from the centre out, mark the blue border, lengthening or shortening the pattern where necessary. Use a ruler to mark a straight line in the middle of the inner border.

3. Assemble the quilt layers together, baste and outline quilt the pieced blocks and continue to quilt as marked.

4. Trim the excess backing and wadding ⅛ inch/3 mm larger than the quilt and baste the edge.

5. Sew binding strips together to make a continuous length. Finish the raw edges using the separate binding method as described in the Techniques section.

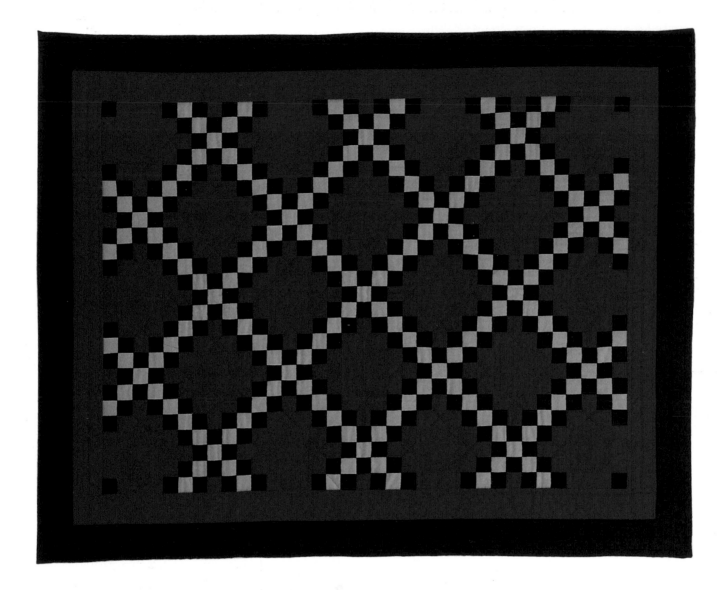

The Double Irish Chain is a simple pattern which uses two blocks to create a chequerboard effect. It can be found in single, double and triple variations. Often seen as coloured chains on a white or cream background, the plain squares provide a perfect space for the skilled needle-woman to display her quilting. This cot-size quilt in the Double-Chain variation is based on a turn-of-the-century Mennonite quilt from Lebanon County, Pennsylvania. The rich and vibrant colours contribute a visual tension and excitement not always found in this normally highly ordered design. If you have never used the strip-cutting method, try it with this project. You will be learning a valuable, new technique which may change the way you make quilts in the future.

DOUBLE IRISH CHAIN

Skill level: Keen intermediate

Finished quilt: 33 × 43 inches / 83.8 × 109.2 cm
Finished block: 5 × 5 inches / 12.7 × 12.7 cm
Number of blocks: 35

MATERIALS

- Red 1¹⁄₃ yards / 1.25 metres
- Yellow ¹⁄₂ yard / 50 cm
- Navy 1¹⁄₂ yards / 1.4 metres
- Wadding 36 × 45 inches / 91.4 × 114.3 cm
- Backing 36 × 45 inches / 91.4 × 114.3 cm

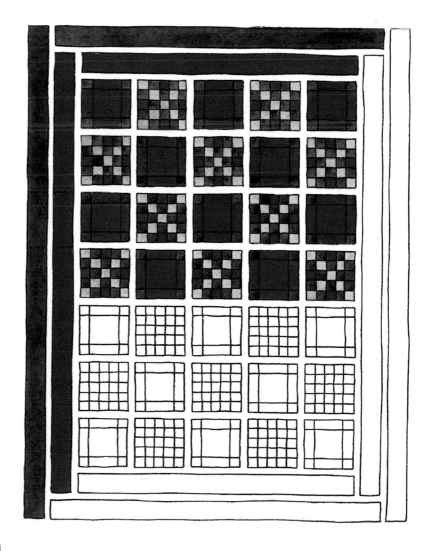

CUTTING INSTRUCTIONS

✂ Measurements for strip lengths are generous to allow for straightening your edges. All measurements include a ¹⁄₄ inch / 6 mm seam allowance.

✂ As you are cutting out, label each set of strips with its dimensions. Pin all the strips of the same measurement together, regardless of colour. This will make it easier to find the correct lengths when making the pieced strips.

Yellow fabric
1. Cut eight strips, 1¹⁄₂ × 32 inches / 3.8 × 81.2 cm.

2. Cut one strip, 1¹⁄₂ × 36 inches / 3.8 × 91.4 cm.

71

Red fabric
1. Cut two strips, $1^{1}/_{2} \times 32$ inches / 3.8×81.2 cm.
2. Cut six strips, $1^{1}/_{2} \times 36$ inches / 3.8×91.4 cm.
3. Cut two strips, $2^{1}/_{2} \times 28$ inches / 6.4×71.1 cm for the border.
4. Cut two strips, $2^{1}/_{2} \times 42$ inches / 6.4×106.6 cm for the border.
5. Cut two strips, $3^{1}/_{2} \times 32$ inches / 8.9×81.2 cm.
6. Cut two strips, $3^{1}/_{2} \times 36$ inches / 8.9×91.4 cm.

Navy fabric
1. Cut 14 strips, $1^{1}/_{2} \times 32$ inches / 3.8×81.2 cm.
2. Cut two strips, $1^{1}/_{2} \times 36$ inches / 3.8×91.4 cm.
3. Cut two strips, $2^{1}/_{2} \times 32$ inches / 6.4×81.2 cm for the border.
4. Cut two strips, $2^{1}/_{2} \times 48$ inches / 6.4×121.9 cm for the border.
5. Cut four strips, 2×42 inches / 5.1×106.6 cm for the binding.

PIECING THE BLOCKS

Block 1

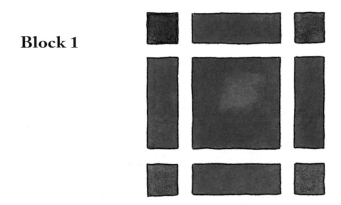

1. Make two pieced-strip units for **Band A** by sewing a navy strip, $1^{1}/_{2} \times 32$ inches / 3.8×81.2 cm to each long edge of a red strip, $3^{1}/_{2} \times 32$ inches / 8.9×81.2 cm. Press the seams towards the navy fabric.

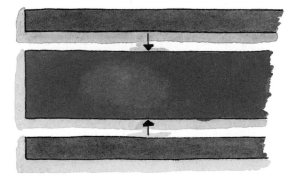

2. Square off one end of each pieced strip. Measuring at $1^{1}/_{2}$ inch / 3.8 cm intervals, cut 36 **Bands A**. Each will measure $1^{1}/_{2} \times 5^{1}/_{2}$ inches / 3.8×14 cm.

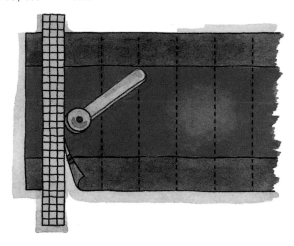

3. Make two pieced-strip units for **Band B** by sewing a narrow red strip, $1^{1}/_{2} \times 36$ inches / 3.8×91.4 cm to each long edge of the red $3^{1}/_{2} \times 36$ inch / 8.9×91.4 cm strip. Press the seams in towards the centre.

4. Square off one end of each pieced strip. Measuring at $3^{1}/_{2}$ inch / 8.9 cm intervals cut 18 **Bands B**. These will measure $3^{1}/_{2} \times 5^{1}/_{2}$ inches / 8.9×14 cm.

5. To complete **Block 1**, sew a **Band A** to the top and bottom of **Band B**. Press the seams towards the navy squares. The block will measure $5^{1}/_{2} \times 5^{1}/_{2}$ inches / 14×14 cm.

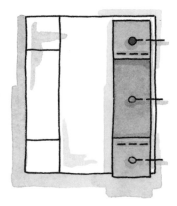

6. Make 17 more blocks following the same sequence.

Block 2

✂ Accurate seam allowances and pressing are especially important when making this block.

1. Sew two pieced strips using yellow, navy and red strips cut to 1¹/₂ × 32 inches / 3.8 × 81.2 cm. Alternate colours as illustrated. After the five coloured strips are sewn together, the width of each pieced strip will measure 5¹/₂ inches / 14 cm. Press all seams towards the navy strips. Grade the seam allowances by trimming away the excess to ¹/₈ inch / 3 mm and fraying one or two threads from the navy fabric.

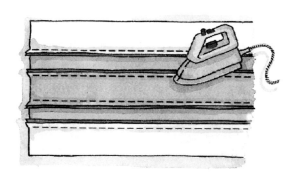

2. Square off one end of each **Pieced strip A** and cut 34 bands at 1¹/₂ inch / 3.8 cm intervals. Each band will measure 1¹/₂ × 5¹/₂ inches / 3.8 × 14 cm.

3. Using the navy and yellow strips cut to 1¹/₂ × 32 inches / 3.8 × 81.2 cm, sew two pieced strips, alternating colours. Each pieced strip will measure 5¹/₂ inches / 14 cm wide. Carefully press the seams towards the navy strips and grade the seams as before.

4. Square off one end of each **Pieced strip B** and cut 34 bands at 1¹/₂ inch / 3.8 cm intervals. Each band will measure 1¹/₂ × 5¹/₂ inches / 3.8 × 14 cm.

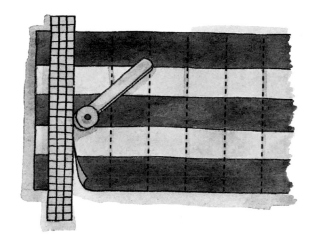

5. Using the red, navy and yellow strips cut to 1¹/₂ × 36 inches / 3.8 × 91.4 cm, sew one pieced strip together alternating colours. The pieced strip will measure 5¹/₂ inches / 14 cm wide. Press the seams towards the navy strips and grade as before.

6. Square off one end of **Pieced strip C** and cut 17 bands at 1¹/₂ inch / 3.8 cm intervals. Each band will measure 1¹/₂ × 5¹/₂ inches / 3.8 × 14 cm.

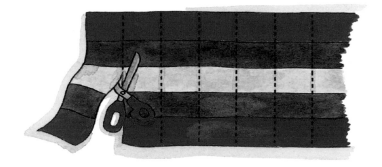

7. To complete **Block 2**, sew the bands together as illustrated. Press the seams open to distribute the bulk evenly. Now make 16 more blocks.

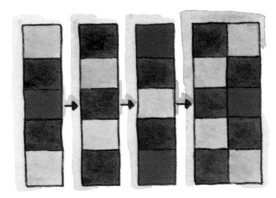

PUTTING THE BLOCKS TOGETHER

1. Sew the blocks together in seven horizontal rows, following the piecing diagram. Press the seam allowances in opposite directions on alternate rows.

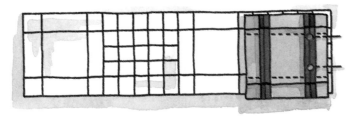

2. Now sew the rows together to make up the quilt top. Press seam allowances open on each of the long rows.

ADDING THE BORDERS

1. Sew the shorter red border strips to the top and bottom of the quilt. Press.

2. Sew the remaining red border strips to the sides. Press.

3. Sew the shorter navy border strips to the top and bottom. Trim if necessary. Press out towards the border.

4. Finally, sew the last two navy border strips to the sides. Press.

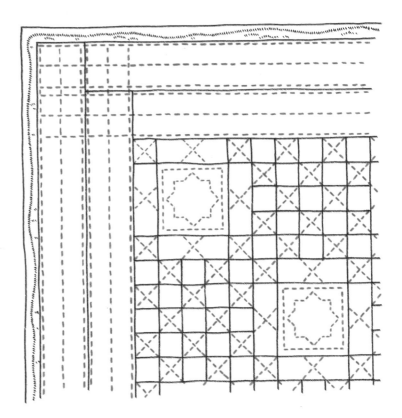

QUILTING & FINISHING

1. Carefully press the quilt top.

2. Using the quilting template supplied, mark the quilting pattern in the centre of each **Block 1**.

3. Assemble the quilt layers and baste. Stitch a last row of basting stitches 3/8 inch/9 mm from the edge of the quilt top.

4. Quilt the blocks and borders as illustrated.

5. Trim excess wadding and backing away to leave a 1/4 inch/6 mm border all around.

6. Sew the binding strips into one continuous length. Follow the instructions for separate binding described in the Techniques section to finish.

TRIP AROUND THE WORLD

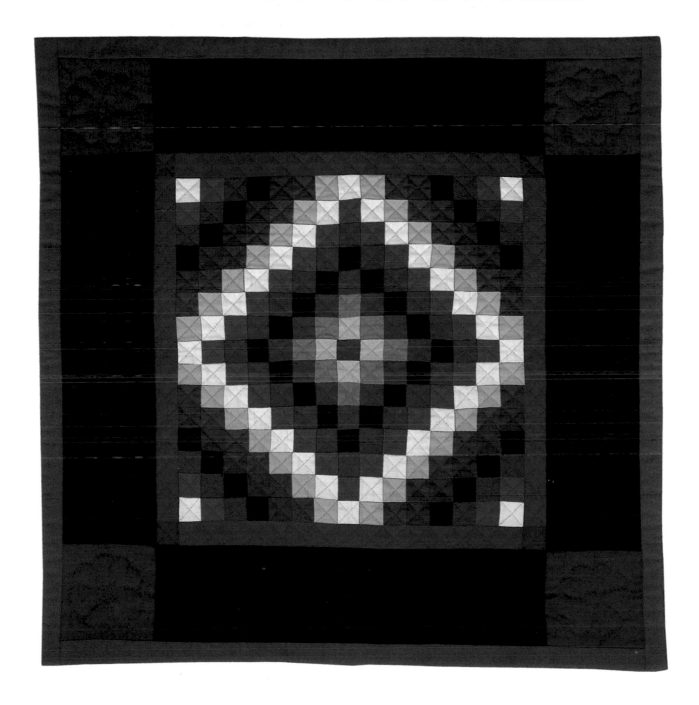

Also known as Sunshine and Shadow, the Trip Around the World pattern is a variation of the simplest of all quilt designs – the one-patch. It is traditionally constructed of concentric squares working outwards from the centre. This small quilt pieced in popular Amish colours – saturated blues, greens, plum and pinks – has been made using a quick-piecing technique. If preferred it can also be sewn by piecing individually cut squares.

TRIP AROUND THE WORLD

Skill level: Confident beginner

Finished quilt: 26 × 26 inches / 66 × 66 cm

COLOUR GUIDE

A	B	C	D	E	F	G	A	G	F	E	D	C	B	A
B	C	D	E	F	G	A	B	A	G	F	E	D	C	B
C	D	E	F	G	A	B	H	B	A	G	F	E	D	C
D	E	F	G	A	B	H	D	H	B	A	G	F	E	D
E	F	G	A	B	H	D	H	D	H	B	A	G	F	E
F	G	A	B	H	D	H	I	H	D	H	B	A	G	F
G	A	B	H	D	H	I	J	I	H	D	H	B	A	G
A	B	H	D	H	I	J	H	J	I	H	D	H	B	A
G	A	B	H	D	H	I	J	I	H	D	H	B	A	G
F	G	A	B	H	D	H	I	H	D	H	B	A	G	F
E	F	G	A	B	H	D	H	D	H	B	A	G	F	E
D	E	F	G	A	B	H	D	H	B	A	G	F	E	D
C	D	E	F	G	A	B	H	B	A	G	F	E	D	C
B	C	D	E	F	G	A	B	A	G	F	E	D	C	B
A	B	C	D	E	F	G	A	G	F	E	D	C	B	A

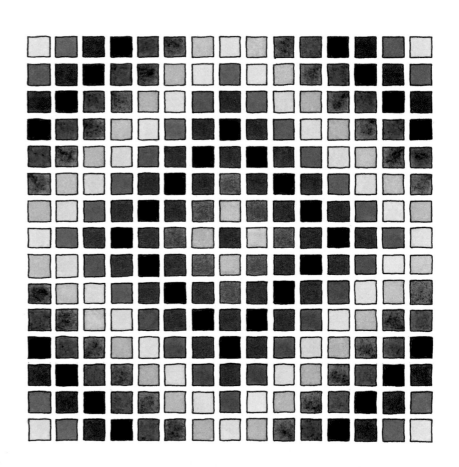

MATERIALS

- (A) Pale pink ¼ yard / 25 cm
- (B) Shocking pink ¼ yard / 25 cm
- (C) Plum ⅛ yard / 15 cm
- (D) Black ½ yard / 50 cm
- (E) Forest green ¼ yard / 25 cm
- (F) Olive green ⅛ yard / 15 cm
- (G) Blue green ¼ yard / 25 cm
- (H) Violet blue ⅜ yard / 40 cm
- (I) Sky blue ⅛ yard / 15 cm
- (J) Ice blue ⅛ yard / 15 cm
- Grey-green for outer border ⅛ yard / 15 cm
- Backing 30 × 30 inches / 76 × 76 cm
- Wadding 30 × 30 inches / 76 × 76 cm

CUTTING INSTRUCTIONS

✂ All measurements include ¼ inch / 6 mm seam allowance. Strip lengths are given longer than required to allow for straightening edges.

1. Iron all fabric scraps.

2. Cut all ten fabrics into 1½ × 8 inch / 3.8 × 20.3 cm long strips:

    8 strips pale pink (A)
    8 strips shocking pink (B)
    3 strips plum (C)
    8 strips black (D)
    5 strips forest green (E)
    6 strips olive green (F)
    7 strips blue green (G)
    8 strips violet blue (H)
    2 strips sky blue (I)
    1 strip ice blue (J)

3. Cut one violet blue (H) square, 1½ × 1½ inches / 3.8 × 3.8 cm for the centre.

4. For the inner border, cut four violet blue (H) strips 1½ × 15½ inches / 3.8 × 39.4 cm. For the corner squares, cut four forest green (E) squares, 1½ × 1½ inches / 3.8 × 3.8 cm.

5. For the middle border, cut four black (D) strips, 4½ × 17½ inches / 11.4 × 29 cm. For the corner squares, cut four forest green (E) squares, 4½ × 4½ inches / 11.4 × 11.4 cm.

6. For the outer border, cut two grey-green strips, 1½ × 25½ inches / 3.8 × 64.8 cm and two grey-green strips, 1½ × 26½ inches / 3.8 × 66.1 cm.

SEWING THE PIECED STRIPS

1. Using a ¼ inch / 6 mm seam allowance, sew strips **A–G** to make **Pieced Strip 1**.

2. To make **Pieced Strip 2**, sew strips **B,C,D,E,F,G** and **A**.

3. To make **Pieced Strip 3**, sew strips **C,D,E,F,G,A** and **B**.

4. To make **Pieced Strip 4**, sew strips **D,E,F,G,A,B** and **H**.

5. To make **Pieced Strip 5**, sew strips **E,F,G,A,B,H** and **D**.

6. To make **Pieced Strip 6**, sew strips **F,G,A,B,H,D** and **H**.

7. To make **Pieced Strip 7**, sew strips **G,A,B,H,D,H** and **I**.

8. To make **Pieced Strip 8**, sew strips **A,B,H,D,H, I,** and **J**.

9. Press all seams open and label each pieced strip from 1–8.

10. Using your ruler, trim the edges straight. Then measure and cut each pieced strip into four 1¹/₂ inch / 3.8 cm bands and label, 1–8.

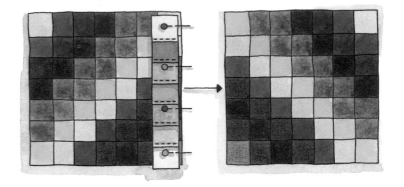

3. Sew the violet blue (H) centre square, between the two remaining **Bands 8** to make one continuous strip.

4. Now, sew the continuous central strip to the top half.

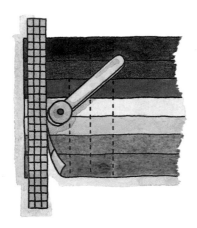

PIECING THE TOP

✂ Take care to match seam allowances at each stage of construction.

1. Using the exploded diagram as a guide, sew **Bands 1–7** to make up the four quarters of the Trip Around the World design.

2. Sew a **Band 8** between the top two quarters to make the top half of the design. Repeat for the bottom half.

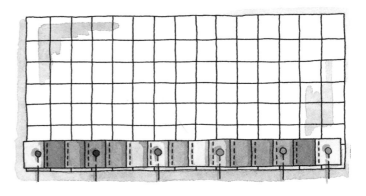

5. Complete the Trip Around the World design by sewing the two halves together.

ADDING THE BORDERS

1. Sew two inner border strips to opposite sides of the central pieced design.

2. Sew a 1½ inch/3.8 cm corner square to each end of the remaining inner borders. Stitch the new border length to the other two sides of the central design.

3. Sew the middle borders onto the pieced central design following the same sequence.

4. Add the outer borders.

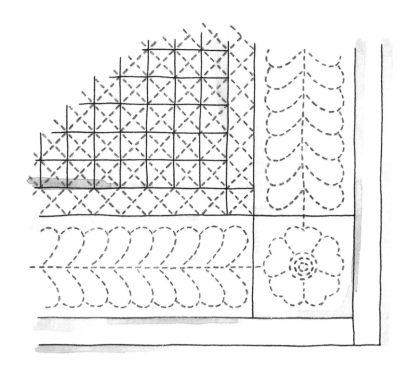

QUILTING & FINISHING

1. Press the quilt top carefully, trimming away any loose threads.

2. Tape the quilt top right side up to a hard, flat surface, and using the quilting templates supplied, mark the quilting patterns. For the middle border, use the feather design and for the four large corner squares, the rose design. Using a ruler mark the central panel with intersecting diagonal lines to achieve a criss-cross effect.

3. Assemble the quilt layers and baste thoroughly.

4. Quilt the central square, borders, and corner blocks as marked. Remove all basting stitches.

5. Trim away the excess wadding and backing to the same size as the quilt top. To bind the quilt, use the fold-finish method. Turn under ¼ inch/6 mm of both the backing and outer border and slipstitch together.

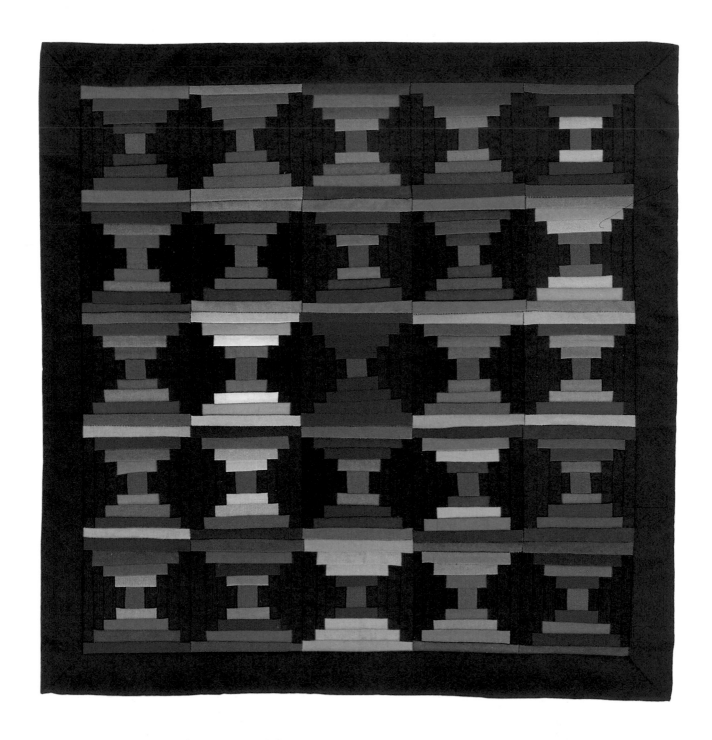

Log cabin style quilts are constructed from narrow strips of cloth arranged around a small central square and sewn to a foundation fabric. There are many log cabin variations and their distinctive patterns are achieved by altering the placement of light and dark strips within each block and by rearranging the block sequence.

COURTHOUSE STEPS

Skill level: Advanced

Finished quilt: $14^{1}/_{2} \times 14^{1}/_{2}$ inches / 37×37 cm
Finished block: $2^{1}/_{2} \times 2^{1}/_{2}$ inches / 6.4×6.4 cm
Number of blocks: 25

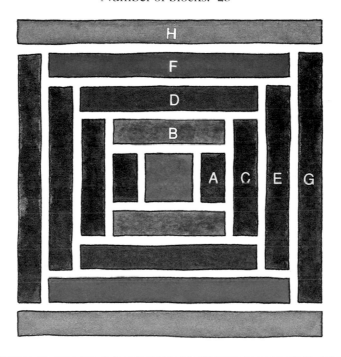

Block colour guide

	Block 1	Block 2	Block 3	Block 4	Block 5
1st Row	forest green (B) mid brown (D) burnt orange (F) blue green (H)	blue (B) mauve (D) dusky pink (F) grey pink (H)	pale blue (B) dull dark green (D) blue green (F) dark forest green (H)	grey green (B) tan (D) mid brown (F) red (H)	bright turquoise (B) red (D) dark purple (F) violet (H)
2nd Row	blue (B) green (D) red (F) medium navy blue (H)	sky blue (B) brilliant orange (D) navy blue (F) sage green (H)	pink (B) dark forest green (D) very dark pink (F) pink (H)	navy blue (B) tan (D) dark forest green (F) bright orange (H)	light violet blue (B) light turquoise (D) bright turquoise (F) sage green (H)
3rd Row	dark blue green (B) green (D) purple blue (F) dusky pink (H)	blue green (B) light yellow (D) bright turquoise (F) dull maize yellow (H)	dark red (B) red (D) bright red (F) pinky red (H)	dull blue green (B) brilliant blue green (D) dusky pink (F) bright turquoise (H)	dull orange (B) brilliant green (D) purple (F) pale blue green (H)
4th Row	blue green (B) grey blue (D) deep pink (F) bright turquoise (H)	yellow (B) grey (D) dusky pink (F) dark purple (H)	bright yellow green (B) red (D) navy blue (F) sky blue (H)	navy blue (B) bright turquoise green (D) bright orange (F) dark red brown (H)	bright forest green (B) dark dull orange (D) pale brown (F) navy blue (H)
5th Row	maize yellow (B) orange (D) khaki green (F) red (H)	light orange (B) dark red brown (D) dull sky blue (F) dark dull pink (H)	red (B) bright turquoise (D) bright green (F) bright turquoise (H)	sky blue (B) grey (D) orange (F) forest green (H)	red (B) sky blue (D) dark red brown (F) khaki green (H)

MATERIALS

✤ Pink ⅛ yard / 15 cm
✤ Black ½ yard / 50 cm
✤ Assorted solid colours ⅓ yard / 30 cm in total
✤ Wadding $18\frac{1}{2} \times 18\frac{1}{2}$ inches / 47 × 47 cm
✤ Backing $18\frac{1}{2} \times 18\frac{1}{2}$ inches / 47 × 47 cm
✤ Tear-away fabric stabiliser (such as Vilene Stitch 'n' Tear)
✤ Fabric glue stick

✂ See the block colour guide if you plan to follow our colour choices. The first colour given is for the log nearest the pink centre square.

CUTTING INSTRUCTIONS

Pink
1. Cut 25 centre squares, 1 × 1 inch / 2.5 × 2.5 cm.

Assorted solid colours
1. The quilt shown here utilises 59 different solid colour fabrics. The wide range of shades adds variety and provides dimension to the finished quilt. Collect as many different colours as you wish for the solid colour logs and cut them into strips, each 1 × 6 inches / 2.5 × 15.5 cm. These can be cut to the correct lengths below as you sew.

    1. For **log B** cut 50 rectangles, $1 \times 1\frac{1}{2}$ inches / 2.5 × 3.8 cm.

    2. For **log D** cut 50 rectangles, 1 × 2 inches / 2.5 × 5.1 cm.

    3. For **log F** cut 50 rectangles, $1 \times 2\frac{1}{2}$ inches / 2.5 × 6.4 cm.

    4. For **log H** cut 50 rectangles, 1 × 3 inches / 2.5 × 7.7 cm.

Black fabric
    1. For **log A** cut 50 squares, 1 × 1 inch / 2.5 × 2.5 cm.

    2. For **log C** cut 50 rectangles, $1 \times 1\frac{1}{2}$ inches / 2.5 × 3.8 cm.

    3. For **log E** cut 50 rectangles, 1 × 2 inches / 2.5 × 5.1 cm.

4. For **log G** cut 50 rectangles, $1 \times 2\frac{1}{2}$ inches / 2.5 × 6.4 cm.

5. For the outer border, cut four strips, $1\frac{1}{2} \times 20\frac{1}{2}$ inches / 3.8 × 52 cm.

Extra length has been allowed for mitring the corners.

Tear-away fabric stabiliser
1. Cut 25 squares, 4 × 4 inches / 10.2 × 10.2 cm..

SEWING THE BLOCKS

✂ Study the exploded diagram to understand the way in which the coloured and black logs work to achieve the distinctive courthouse steps pattern.

1. Trace the block pattern below and tape it to your work surface. Then tape a square of fabric stabiliser over your tracing. Accurately trace 25 blocks including the broken line which represents your cutting line.

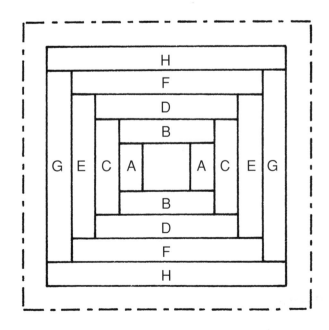

2. Centre a pink square right side up, on the unmarked side of the foundation. Keep it from moving by sticking it with fabric glue. Hold it up to the light to ensure it is correctly positioned.

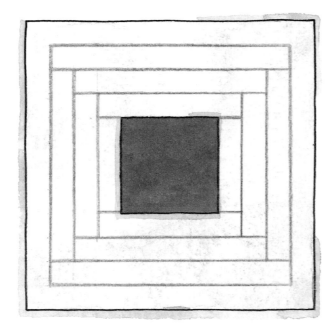

3. Place a square **black log A** over the centre pink square, right sides together. Turn the foundation over carefully to the marked side while holding the log in place. Sew directly on the marked line between the **centre square** and **log A**. (The fabric logs will be underneath the foundation.) Start and end two or three stitches beyond the seam line.

4. Turn the foundation over to the unmarked side and trim away the excess seam allowance so that the fabric does not extend into the next parallel seam.

5. Finger press the seam open so that the **black log A** lies flat. Press firmly with a dry iron. Trim **log A** so that it is now exactly ¹/₂ inch / 1.3 cm wide.

6. Repeat Steps 3 through 5 with another **black log A**, on the opposite side of the pink centre.

7. Continue adding to the foundation around the pink centre in alphabetical order, alternating a coloured pair of logs with a black pair of logs. Remember to trim down seam allowances after each step.

3. Press seams to one side with a dry iron and trim away excess foundation fabric. Alternate the direction of pressed seams with each horizontal row.

4. Join the horizontal rows, matching seam allowances, to make up the quilt top. Press seams in the same direction.

ADDING THE BORDERS

1. Pin, then sew, the black border strips to opposite sides of the quilt starting and stopping $1/4$ inch / 6 mm from the raw edges. Sew the remaining strips to the top and bottom in the same way. Follow the instructions for mitred borders in the Techniques section.

8. Press completed blocks with a dry iron. Square up the edges by trimming each block to the outer cutting line on the foundation.

FINISHING

1. As this quilt requires no quilting do not remove the fabric stabiliser. Press the quilt top carefully, trimming away all loose threads.

PUTTING THE BLOCKS TOGETHER

1. Lay out the blocks on a flat surface five across and five down. Turn the blocks so that the coloured logs run horizontally. Study the photograph of the quilt if you need guidance.

2. Pin, then sew five horizontal rows of blocks together in the correct order. Make sure that you match stitching lines between blocks. When sewing black seams together, make sure to use black thread.

2. Because this quilt is constructed on foundation fabric, it does not require quilting. Assemble the quilt layers and pin baste together.

3. Trim away excess backing and wadding to the same size as the quilt top. Use the fold-finish method to bind the quilt, as described in the Techniques section. Turn under $1/4$ inch / 6 mm of both the backing and outer border and slipstitch together. Remove basting pins.

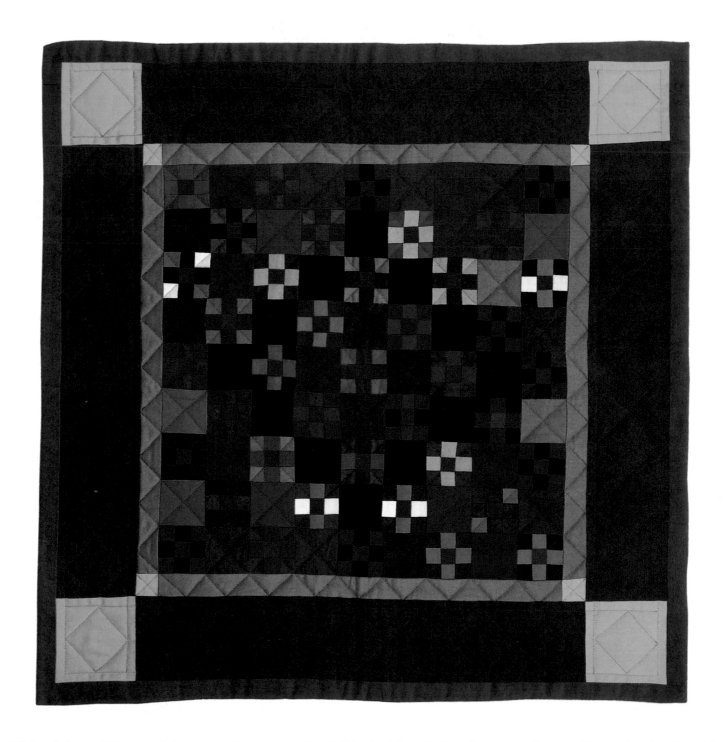

This miniature Nine-patch is a copy of an outstanding 1920s Amish quilt from Lancaster County, Pennsylvania. Pieced from a vibrant palette of saturated colours, it is typical of the dramatic colour scheme favoured by Amish quilters. The quilt's vitality comes from the variety of shades used within several colour families. Common to all the pieced blocks is the central red accent. A secondary pattern is created by the placement of black setting blocks which form a diamond within the square.

NINE-PATCH

Skill level: Beginner

Finished quilt: 22 × 22 inches / 55.8 × 55.8 cm
Finished block: 1½ inches / 3.8 cm
Number of blocks: 41 pieced and 40 plain

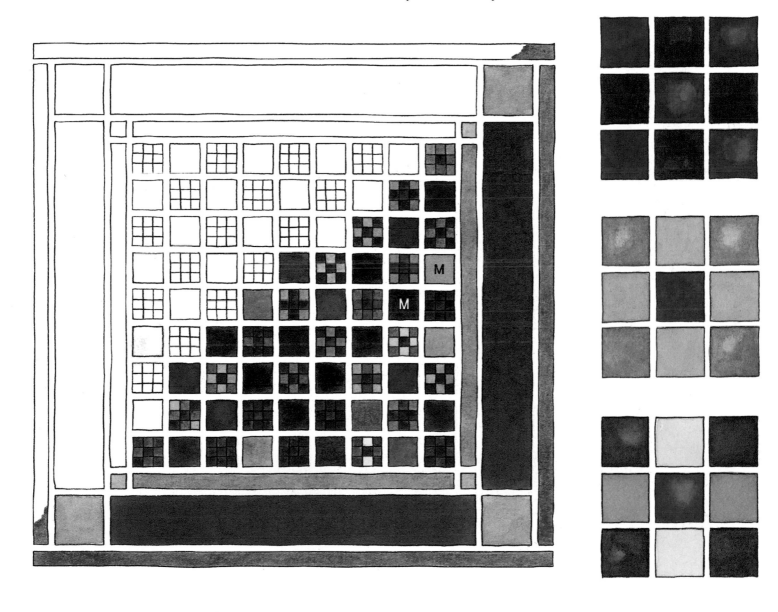

MATERIALS

- Black ¹/₈ yard / 15 cm
- Red (**3 shades**) each 6 ¹/₂ × 18 inches / 16.5 × 45.7 cm
- Pink 1 scrap 6 ¹/₂ × 6 ¹/₂ inches / 16.5 × 16.5 cm
- Purple (**3 shades**) each 6 ¹/₂ × 6 ¹/₂ inches / 16.5 × 6.5 cm
- Brown (**3 shades**) each 4 ¹/₂ × 6 ¹/₂ inches / 11.4 × 16.5 cm
- Blue (**3 shades** to include navy, bright and pale blue) each 6 ¹/₂ × 6 ¹/₂ inches / 16.5 × 16.5 cm
- Green (**2 shades**) ¹/₄ yd / 25 cm
- Orange 1 scrap 2 ¹/₂ × 6 ¹/₂ inches / 6.4 × 16.5 cm
- Cream or yellow 1 scrap 4 × 6 ¹/₂ inches / 10.2 × 16.5 cm
- Turquoise for posts ¹/₈ yard / 15 cm
- Purple for middle border ¹/₄ yard / 25 cm
- Dark sage green for outer border ¹/₄ yard / 25 cm
- Wadding 26 × 26 inches / 66 × 66 cm
- Backing 26 × 26 inches / 66 × 66 cm
- Transparent nylon thread for machine-quilting

CUTTING INSTRUCTIONS

1. Using **Template M**, cut out 40 squares, 2 × 2 inches / 5.1 × 5.1 cm in the following colours: 12 black, eight purples, nine reds, three browns, three oranges, two greens, two bright blue and one navy blue.

2. **For the Nine-patch blocks, use the strip-cutting technique**: Cut strips 1 inch / 2.5 cm wide and at least 6 inches / 15.2 cm long in an assortment of colours. The number of strips to cut for each colour depends on your colour combinations. Make sure you have plenty of reds, some purple and black strips ready for sewing.

3. For the inner border, cut four strips, 1¹/₄ × 14 inches / 3.2 × 35.6 cm from the sage green fabric. Next, cut four turquoise squares, 1¹/₄ × 1¹/₄ inches / 3.2 × 3.2 cm for the corner posts.

4. For the middle border, cut four purple strips, 3¹/₄ × 15 ¹/₂ inches / 8.3 × 39.4 cm. For the corner posts, cut four turquoise squares, 3¹/₄ × 3¹/₄ inches / 8.3 × 8.3 cm.

5. For the outer border, cut two strips, 1¹/₄ × 21 inches / 3.2 × 55.7 cm and two strips, 1¹/₄ × 23 inches / 3.2 × 58.4 cm from the dark sage green fabric.

PIECING THE BLOCKS

✂ Be sure to use an accurate ¹/₄ inch / 6 mm seam allowance throughout.

✂ All the Nine-patch blocks in this quilt have a red centre. Some of the blocks are made up of red and one other colour, and some of red and two other colours.

To piece a Nine-patch block with two colours:

1. Sew a pieced strip using red in the centre and one other colour of your choice on either side. Press seams towards the centre.

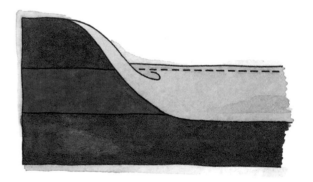

2. Sew a second pieced strip reversing the colours. Press towards the red strips.

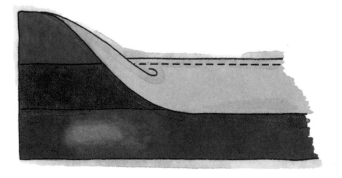

3. Cut the pieced strips into 1 inch / 2.5 cm bands.

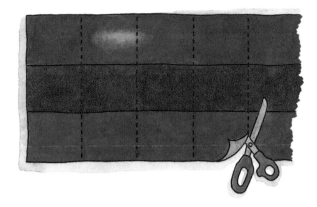

4. Matching seams carefully, sew the bands in the correct order to make the Nine-patch block.

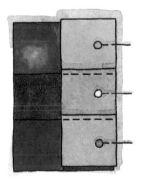

To piece a Nine-patch block with three colours:

1. Select three strips, two of one colour and one of a different colour. Sew the strips together with the odd colour in the middle. Press seams towards the outer strips.

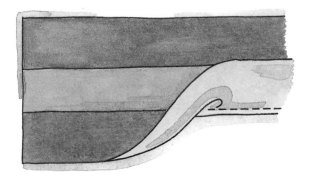

2. Sew a second pieced strip using red as the centre colour. Use the same colour for the outer strips as chosen for the middle of the first strip set. Press towards the centre strip.

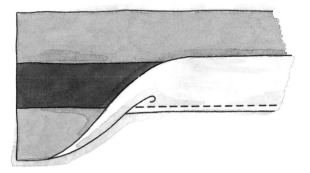

3. Cut the pieced strips into 1 inch / 2.5 cm bands.

4. Sew the bands into a Nine-patch block as before, matching seams carefully.

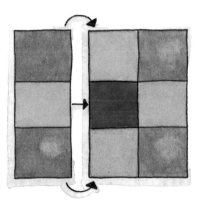

To piece a Nine-patch block with four colours:

1. Make up one pieced strip using two different colours.

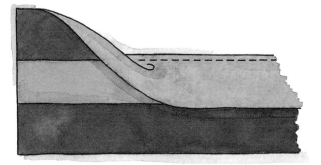

2. Make a second strip using two more colours.

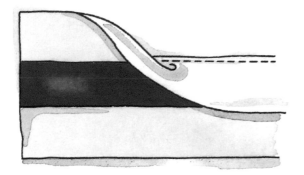

3. Cut the pieced strips into bands at 1 inch / 2.5 cm intervals. Remember when sewing the bands together to reverse one of the outside bands.

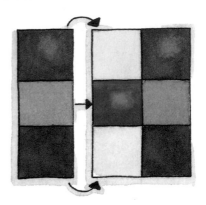

PUTTING THE BLOCKS TOGETHER

1. Press the blocks and trim any loose threads.

2. Lay out the Nine-patch blocks and alternate with plain blocks. Refer to the quilt plan for placement of the black blocks to form the central diamond. Pin, then sew the blocks together into horizontal rows. Press seam allowances on even number rows to the right and odd rows to the left so that blocks will align precisely.

3. Sew the rows together, matching seam allowances, to complete the central design.

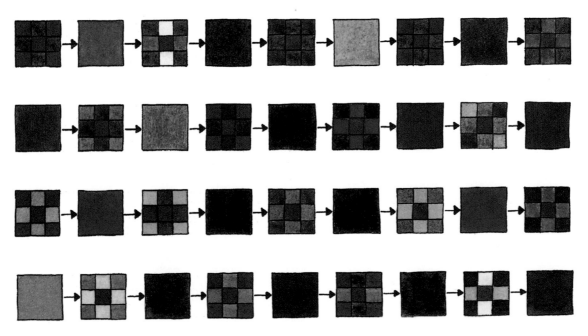

ADDING THE BORDERS

1. Sew two inner border strips to opposite sides of the central design.

2. Sew the small turquoise squares to the two remaining inner border strips. Sew these borders to the top and bottom of the quilt.

3. Sew middle borders and large turquoise squares to the central design following the same sequence.

4. Sew the 21 inch / 53.3 cm outer border strips to opposite sides of the quilt. Press out.

5. Sew the remaining strips to the top and bottom in the same way.

QUILTING & FINISHING

1. Press the quilt top and remove any loose threads. Assemble the quilt layers and baste.

2. To overcome the difficulty of matching quilting thread to a multi-coloured top, thread your sewing machine with transparent nylon thread. Use cotton thread in your bobbin. Machine-quilt in diagonal lines through the centre of each square and extend into the inner border. This will give a criss-cross effect.

3. Machine-quilt ¼ inch / 6 mm inside the seams of the middle border. Finally, inside the purple borders, quilt diagonal lines 1½ inches / 3.8 cm apart to create 'squares on point'. Remove all basting stitches.

4. Trim away the excess backing and wadding to the same size as the quilt top. To use the fold-finish method to bind the quilt, turn under ¼ inch / 6 mm of both the backing and binding and slipstitch together.

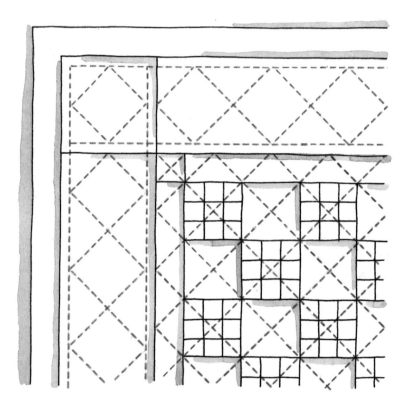

Scrap Quilts

Crazy Quilt

Lemoyne Star

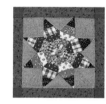

Country Plaids

Kate's House

A crazy quilt offers an opportunity to use all sorts of exotic fabrics. They must be chosen carefully, with colours organised to include both a variety of tones within the same colour family and an interesting range of textures to create the 'crazy' look. The embroidery and other embellishments can be as bold or as subtle as you like, and can be done by machine. Most sewing machines today have a range of stitches that can replicate some of the amazing embroidery found on Victorian crazy quilts.

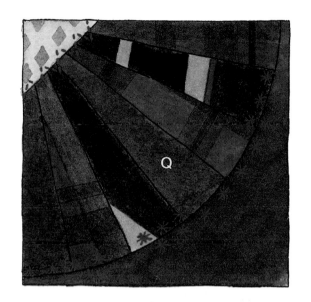

CRAZY QUILT

Skill level: Beginner

Finished quilt: 22 × 22 inches / 55.9 × 55.9 cm
Finished block: 3¹/₂ × 3¹/₂ inches / 8.9 × 8.9 cm
Number of blocks: 25

MATERIALS

❖ Assorted silks, satins, velvets, taffetas, ribbons, brocades and upholstery samples   1 yard / 1 metre in total
❖ Dark taffeta scraps for foundation of corner fan blocks ¹/₈ yard / 15 cm
❖ Pre-washed, light-weight cotton for the foundation squares ¹/₂ yard / 50 cm
❖ Black cotton velvet ¹/₄ yard / 25 cm for border

❖ Backing 25 × 25 inches / 62.8 × 62.8 cm
❖ Wadding 25 × 25 inches / 62.8 × 62.8 cm
❖ Black taffeta ¹/₄ yard / 25 cm for binding
❖ 2 spools machine embroidery thread in a contrasting colour
❖ Strips of furnishing braid for embellishment (optional)
❖ Fabric glue stick
❖ One skein pearl cotton for tying

CUTTING INSTRUCTIONS

✂ Separate scraps into darks, mediums and lights. Using a dry iron, press all fabrics before cutting.

Crazy blocks
1. Cut 21 squares, $4^{1}/_2 \times 4^{1}/_2$ / 11.4 × 11.4 cm from the muslin for the foundation blocks.
2. Do not cut any scraps for the blocks until you are ready to sew.

Corner fan blocks
1. Using **Template Q**, trace and cut a total of 28 wedges from a mixture of heavy silks and taffetas. Each of the four blocks requires seven pieces. Remember to add $^{1}/_4$ inch / 6 mm seam allowance as you cut.

2. Cut four squares, $4^{1}/_2 \times 4^{1}/_2$ inches / 11.4 × 11.4 cm from the dark taffeta for the foundation of the fans.

3. From a bright scrap, cut one square 3×3 inches / 7.6 × 7.6 cm. Cut across both diagonals to make four triangles. Use these pieces for the base of each fan block.

Borders and binding
1. For the black velvet border, cut two strips, $2^{1}/_4 \times 18$ inches / 5.7 × 45.7 cm and two strips, $2^{1}/_4 \times 21^{1}/_2$ inches / 5.7 × 54.6 cm.
2. For the binding, cut two strips, 2 inches / 5.1 cm wide across the full width of the black taffeta.

SEWING THE BLOCKS

✂ Most crazy quilts are constructed using a method where fabric pieces are sewn to cover a foundation square. Each fabric, except for the first, is simply straight-stitched to the foundation with each new piece covering the raw edges of the previous.

Crazy blocks
1. Select six to eight fabric scraps for each of the 21 crazy blocks. Cut scraps into a variety of straight-sided shapes.

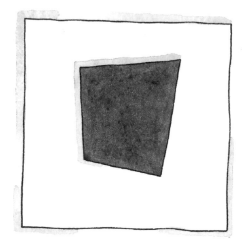

2. Place one of the scraps in the middle of a foundation square. Use a little fabric glue to secure it.

3. Position the second scrap along the edge of the first with right sides together. Sew a $^{1}/_4$ inch / 6 mm seam through all layers. Trim the seam allowance down to $^{3}/_{16}$ inch / 4 mm. Fold out and press the second patch open to overlap the foundation.

4. Add additional patches, alternating colours and textures, until the foundation square is completely covered.

5. Trim off the overlapping fabric by cutting the foundation square down to 4 × 4 inches / 10.2 × 10.2 cm. This is most easily done with a rotary cutter, but traditional scissors are perfectly adequate.

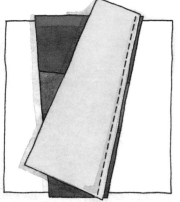 

6. Make a further 20 crazy blocks in the same way.

Corner fan blocks

1 Select seven wedges and sew them together using matching thread.

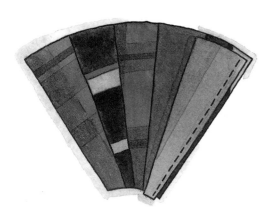

2. Press the seams to one side.

3. Fit the prepared fan into one corner of a dark taffeta foundation square. Use a little fabric glue to hold it in place.

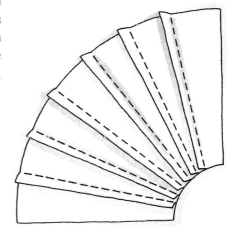

4. With right sides facing, pin then sew a triangle to cover the corner of the fan.

5. Baste the raw edges of the fan to the foundation block. Leave the curved edge unfinished as it will be covered by machine or hand embroidery.

6. Trim the block down to 4 × 4 inches / 10.2 × 10.2 cm.

7. Make three more fan blocks following the same sequence.

EMBELLISHING THE BLOCKS

✂ Using machine embroidery thread, embroider each block using a variety of stitches. Study the photograph of the quilt carefully for ideas or look at pictures of old crazy quilts. Embellish each block in any way you wish. Use furnishing braid, ribbons, upholstery trimmings, and buttons to enrich the blocks. Another interesting surface treatment is to appliqué floral motifs, butterflies and birds cut from furnishing fabric onto the blocks.

PUTTING THE BLOCKS TOGETHER

1. Lay out the crazy blocks on a flat surface, alternating dark and light. Move the blocks around until you achieve a balance of colour and texture. Place a fan block in each corner, making sure to turn the block in its correct orientation.

2. Pin, then sew the blocks together in order to make five rows with five blocks in each row.

3. Sew the rows together to complete the quilt top. Press lightly with a dry iron and a pressing cloth.

4. Machine embroider over all the seams on the quilt top.

ADDING THE BORDER

1. Sew the 18 inch / 45.7 cm velvet strips to the sides of the quilt. Press with a dry iron using a pressing cloth.

2. Sew the longer velvet borders to the top and bottom. Press with a dry iron.

TYING & FINISHING

1. Assemble the quilt layers and baste together.

2. Finish the top by tying with embroidery thread. However, instead of bringing the ties through to the right side, tie the quilt at the back.

3. Sew the taffeta binding strips into a continuous length. Press in half lengthwise, and then press each raw edge into the centre fold line. Matching raw edges, pin then sew the binding to the front of the quilt using a $^1/_2$ inch / 1.3 cm seam allowance.

4. Bring the black taffeta binding over to the back of the quilt and slipstitch the fold to the backing of the quilt.

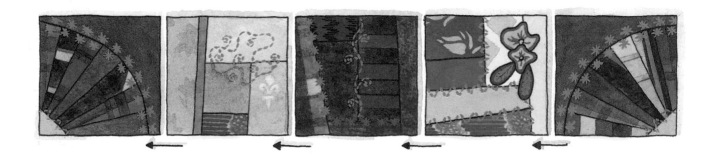

LEMOYNE STAR

It has been said that the art of patchwork is really history through the eye of a needle. Nowhere is this truer than in the Lemoyne Star pattern. In New England, they called it Lemon Star and little knew or cared that they were stitching a part of the crest of John Baptiste Le Moyne, Sieur de Bienville, the founder a century earlier of New Orleans. In this strip and scrap version of the Lemoyne Star, the segments are cut from pieced fabric made by sewing strips of random widths to a foundation. Strips are cut across the full width of 100% cotton prints, checks and stripes. To use strips cut from small scraps, simply sew them to smaller pieces of foundation fabric to make a piece large enough to cut one or more segments of the star.

LEMOYNE STAR

Skill level: Intermediate

Finished quilt: 25 × 25 inches / 63.5 × 63.5 cm
Finished block: 6 × 6 inches / 15.2 × 15.2 cm
Number of blocks: 9

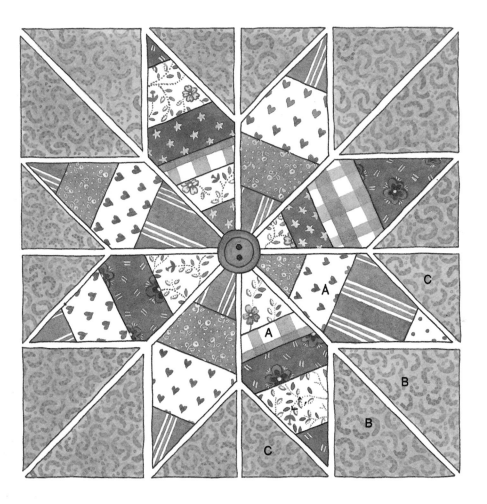

MATERIALS

- Lightweight cotton for foundation fabric one square 20 × 20 inches / 50.8 × 50.8 cm
- Assorted dark prints ⅛ yard / 15 cm **each** of 10–15 predominantly blue fabrics with touches of white, russet and gold
- Assorted light prints ⅛ yard / 15 cm **each** of 4–5 predominantly white and cream fabrics with blue highlights
- Gold print for background ½ yard / 50 cm

- Russet print for sashing ⅓ yard / 30 cm
- Blue print for border and binding ⅓ yard / 30 cm
- Solid blue for posts ¼ yard / 25 cm
- Backing 28 × 28 inches / 71.1 × 71.1 cm
- Wadding 28 × 28 inches / 71.1 × 71.1 cm
- 9 buttons ¾ inch / 19 mm diameter

CUTTING INSTRUCTIONS

✄ Templates are provided if you prefer to use traditional cutting methods. Where measurements are given for quick-cutting, seam allowances are included.

Assorted dark and light prints
1. Cut three to four strips from each fabric in widths ranging from $^3/_4$–$1^1/_4$ inches / 1.9–3.2 cm.

Gold fabric
1. Cut 36 squares, $2^5/_8 \times 2^5/_8$ inches / 6.7 × 6.7 cm. Cut in half on the diagonal to make 72 **B triangles**.
2. Cut 18 squares, 3×3 inches / 7.6 × 7.6 cm. Cut across both diagonals to make 72 **C triangles**.

Russet fabric
1. Cut four strips, $1^1/_2$ inches / 3.8 cm wide across the full width of the fabric. From each strip cut six **E** sashing pieces, $1^1/_2 \times 6^1/_2$ inches / 3.8 × 16.5 cm.

Blue print
1. Cut four strips, $1^3/_4 \times 29$ inches / 4.4 × 73.7 cm for the border. Extra length has been given for mitring the corners.
2. For the binding, cut three strips, $1^1/_2$ inches / 3.8 cm across the full width of the fabric.

Solid blue fabric
1. For the posts, cut 16 **D squares**, $1^1/_2 \times 1^1/_2$ inches / 3.8 × 3.8 cm.

SEWING THE FOUNDATION FABRIC

1. To make up the strippy fabric, sew the strips onto the foundation fabric at random, alternating light, medium and dark blue prints with the white or cream prints. The random widths and uneven seam allowances contribute to the haphazard look of the Lemoyne Stars. Set your stitch length to 10–12 stitches per 1 inch / 2.5 cm to reduce the chance of fraying.

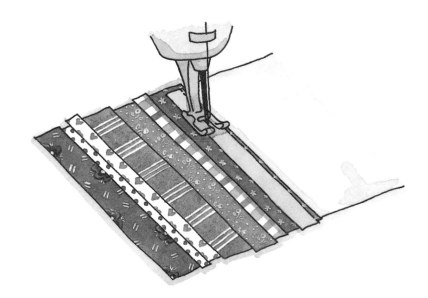

2. Using **Template A**, cut a total of 72 star segments from your strippy fabric.

PIECING THE BLOCKS

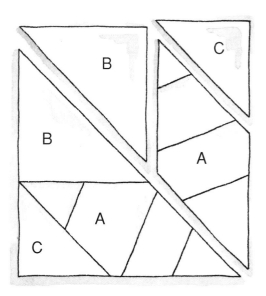

1. Referring to the quarter block plan, sew a **B** and **C triangle** to an **A star segment**. Press seam allowances towards the gold fabric.

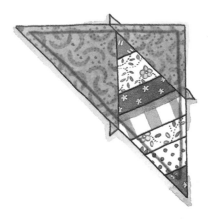

2. Sew the mirror image of the unit made above by reversing the position of the **B** and **C triangles** on another **A star segment**.

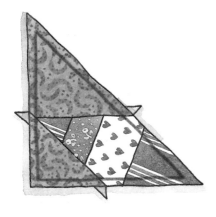

3. Sew these two units together to form one quarter of the Lemoyne Star block. Press the seam allowance open.

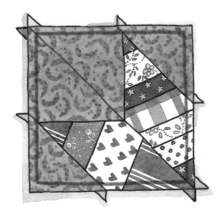

4. Repeat the sequence to form the second quarter of the block. Sew both quarters together to form half the Lemoyne Star.

5. Construct the other half of the Lemoyne Star in the same way. Sew both halves together to complete one block. Press seam allowance open. Sew nine blocks in all.

PUTTING THE BLOCKS TOGETHER

1. Sew three blocks and four sashing strips together as illustrated to make a horizontal row. Press seams towards the sashing strips.

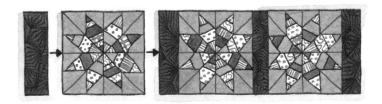

2. Sew two more rows of alternating blocks and sashing strips.

3. Sew four **D posts** to three sashing strips to make a pieced horizontal sashing strip. Press seams towards the sashing strips. Make three more.

4. Sew the four horizontal sashing strips to the three rows of Lemoyne Stars to complete the pieced top. Press all seams towards the sashing strips.

ADDING THE BORDERS

1. Starting from the centre, pin then sew border strips to opposite sides of the quilt. Sew border strips on, beginning and ending your seam ¼ inch / 6 mm away from each edge. Press borders out.

2. Sew the remaining borders to the top and bottom without stitching over the side borders. Allow the excess border to overhang.

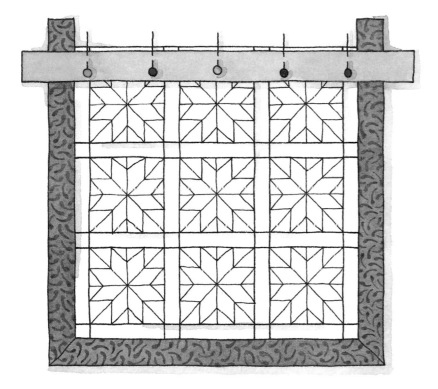

3. Follow the instructions in the Techniques section to mitre the corners.

QUILTING & FINISHING

1. Press the quilt top carefully.

2. On a flat surface, layer the backing, wadding and quilt top as directed in the Techniques section. Pin and baste securely.

3. Quilt in-the-ditch on all four diagonal seam lines of the Lemoyne Star. Outline quilt the gold corner squares and triangles.

4. For the border, quilt a straight line one inch / 2.5 cm from the raw edge of the quilt top, and in-the-ditch between the border and sashing seams.

5. Trim the backing and wadding ⅛ inch / 3 mm larger than the quilt top and baste the edge.

6. Join the binding strips to make a continuous length. Finish the raw edges of the quilt according to the instructions for separate binding in the Techniques section.

7. Sew a button at the centre of each star to finish the quilt.

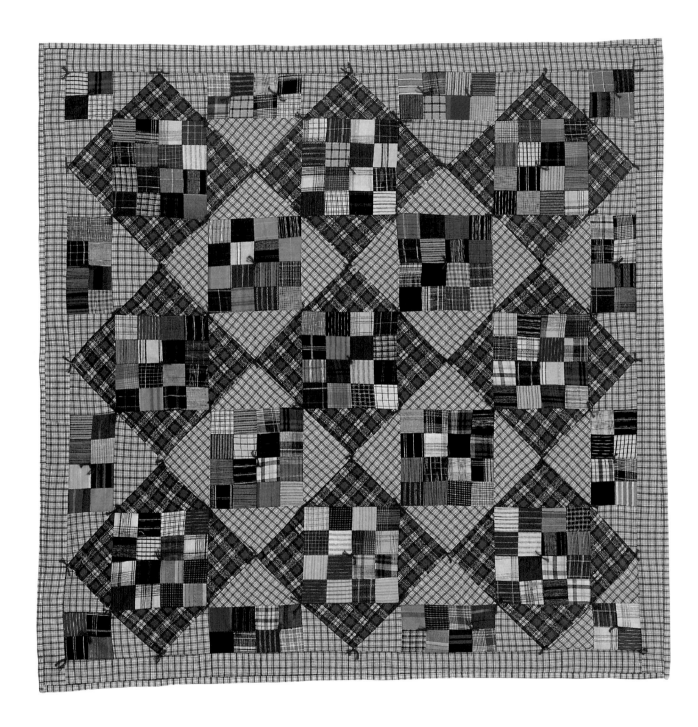

Most quilters have a good supply of die-cut samples that they have collected over the years from mail-order fabric companies. The design of this quilt is ideal for using these and any cotton scraps. Before you begin cutting and piecing the scrap blocks, sort your swatches into darks, mediums and lights. Then, make your selection to include a wide variety of colour, tone and contrast. Choose the two fabrics for the dominant Blocks B and E, so that they set off the randomness of the scrap blocks.

COUNTRY PLAIDS

Skill level: Beginner

Finished quilt: 33 × 33 inches / 84 × 84 cm
Finished block: 5 × 5 inches / 13 × 13 cm
Number of blocks: 25 blocks

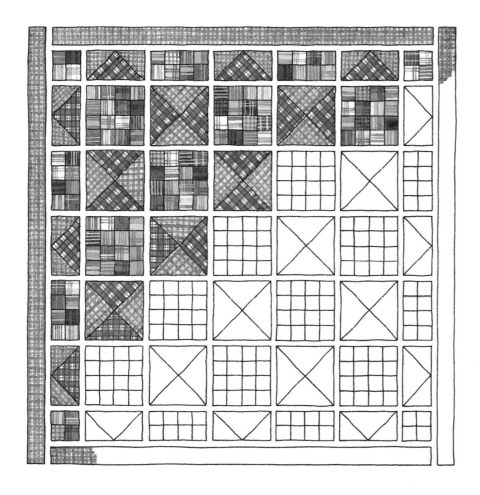

16-patch Block A

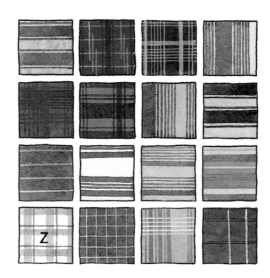

Four-patch Block B

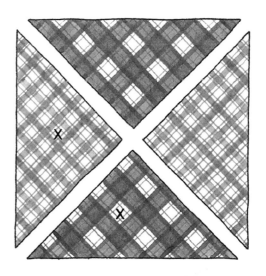

Block C

Block D

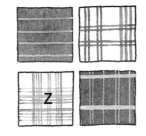

Flying Geese Block E

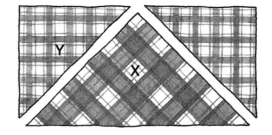

MATERIALS

- 288 assorted squares in plaids and stripes, at least 1³/₄ × 1³/₄ inches / 5 × 5 cm
- Dark plaid ¹/₂ yard / 50 cm
- Light plaid ³/₄ yard / 75 cm for border and binding
- Backing 36 × 36 inches / 91.4 × 91.4 cm
- Wadding 36 × 36 inches / 91.4 × 91.4 cm
- One skein pearl cotton for tying

CUTTING INSTRUCTIONS

Dark plaid fabric
1. Cut nine squares, 6¹/₄ × 6¹/₄ inches / 15.8 × 15.8 cm. Cut across both diagonals to make 36 triangles (**Template X**). Set aside and label 24 for **Block B**, and 12 for **Block E**.

Light plaid fabric
1. Cut six squares 6¹/₄ × 6¹/₄ / 15.9 × 15.9 cm. Cut across both diagonals to make 24 triangles (**Template X**) for **Block B**.

2. Cut 12 squares, 3³/₈ × 3³/₈ inches / 8.6 × 8.6 cm. Then cut in half diagonally to make 24 triangles (**Template Y**) for **Block E**.

3. For the borders cut two strips, 2 × 32 inches / 5.1 × 81.3 cm and two strips, 2 × 35 inches / 5.1 × 88.9 cm.

4. For the binding, cut four strips 1¹/₄ inch / 3.2 cm wide across the full width of the fabric.

Assorted squares
✂ You will need a total of 288 squares to make up **Blocks A, C** and **D**. If you are using die-cut fabric samples, make sure that each is a perfect 1³/₄ inch / 4.4 cm square, by checking with either a ruler or **Template Z**. Discard any squares that are too small to be straightened.

✂ If you are using larger scraps, press then cut three or four at a time using **Template Z** as a guide.

PIECING THE BLOCKS

Block A

1. Using the 1³/₄ inch / 4.5 cm squares, make up 13 blocks with 16 squares in each block. Try to achieve a balance of colour in each block. Sew the squares together in units of four, alternating dark with light, or dark with medium squares.

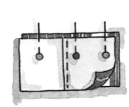

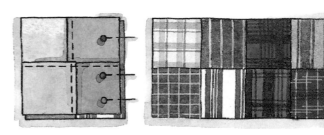
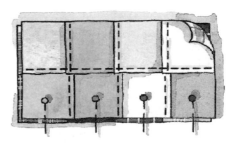

Block C

1. Make up eight blocks with eight squares in each block.

Block D

1. Make up four blocks with four squares in each block.

Block E

1. Set a **Y triangle** to one of the shorter sides of an **X triangle**. Sew along the diagonal edge as illustrated. Open out the triangles, pressing the seam allowances to the darker fabric.

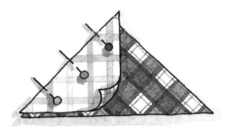

2. Set the second **Y triangle** in the bottom corner, making sure that the top point is off-set by ¹/₄inch/6 mm. Sew along the diagonal edge, making sure that the seams intersect ¹/₄inch/6mm from the top edge. Open out the triangles and press.

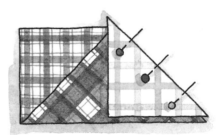

3. Make 11 more **E Blocks**.

Block B

1. Using two **X triangles** from each fabric, piece 12 blocks by joining alternate triangles to make a square.

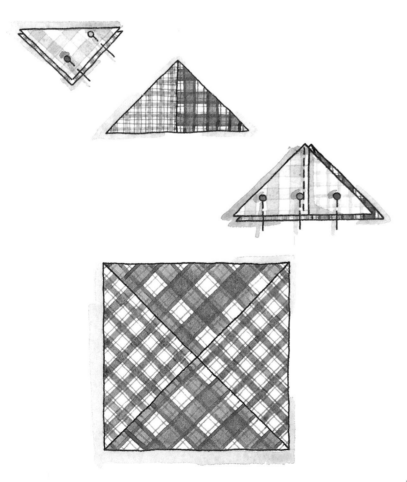

PUTTING THE BLOCKS TOGETHER

1. Make up **Row 1** by sewing blocks together in the following sequence: **Blocks D, E, C, E, C, E** and **D.** Make sure that the **E Blocks** are turned according to the quilt layout. Press seam allowances to the left.

2. Make up **Rows 2, 4** and **6** by sewing blocks together in the following sequence: **Blocks E, A, B, A, B, A** and **E.** Note that the orientation of **Block B** changes between rows. Press seam allowances to the right.

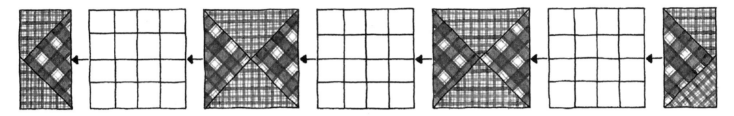

3. Make up **Rows 3** and **5** by sewing together **Blocks C, B, A, B, A, B** and **C.** Press seam allowances towards the left.

4. Make up **Row 7** by sewing the same block sequence as used to make **Row 1.** Remember to invert the three **E Blocks** so that the point of the triangle faces out to the border.

5. Pin, then sew **Rows 1–7** together. Because the seam allowances have been pressed in alternating directions, the rows will 'lock' together precisely.

ADDING THE BORDER

1. Check the measurement of the sides of the quilt to determine the exact lengths for the side border strips. Trim them accordingly.

2. Pin, then sew the border strips to the top and bottom of the quilt top. Press seam allowances towards the borders.

3. Trim the side border strips to the exact length of the quilt top. Include in your measurement the borders you have just sewn. Sew in place and press.

TYING & FINISHING

1. Press the pieced top carefully and trim away all loose threads which may show through to the front.

2. Assemble the quilt layers and pin baste.

3. Use pearl cotton to tie the centre and corners of each block according to the instructions in the Techniques section.

4. Trim away excess backing and wadding $1/8$ inch / 3 mm larger than the quilt top.

5. Sew binding strips together to make one length and finish the raw edges of the quilt using the continuous binding technique.

KATE'S HOUSE

Reminiscent of early folk art, this quaint picture of a house, garden and oversized birds, has been pieced with a colourful assortment of prints, plaids and stripes to create the simplicity and cheerfulness associated with children's art. This quilt picture is sewn using a combination of piecing and appliqué techniques. The completed units are joined in sequence and then quilted. The inner border is made using a quick strip-piecing technique combined with single squares to give a random effect.

KATE'S HOUSE

Skill level: Confident beginner

Finished quilt: $18^1/2 \times 17^1/2$ inches / 47×44.5 cm
Appliquéd central panel: $13^1/2 \times 12^1/2$ inches / 34.3×31.8 cm

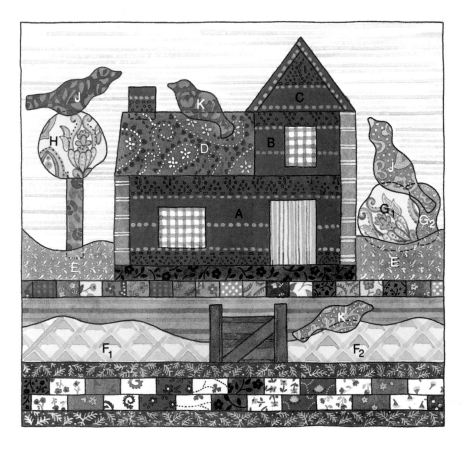

MATERIALS

- ❖ Red print for house, gables and chimney $^1/4$ yard / 25 cm
- ❖ Assorted blue prints, stripes and checks for sides of house, roof, windows, birds and gate $^1/3$ yard / 30 cm
- ❖ Assorted brown prints and stripes for door, base and foreground of house, garden wall and tree trunk $^1/4$ yard / 25 cm
- ❖ Assorted shades of green for hedges, bushes and tree $^1/4$ yard / 25 cm
- ❖ 25 assorted scraps for 'flower' and pieced inner borders 4×12 inches / 10.2×30.5 cm **each**
- ❖ 13 assorted light, medium and dark scraps for garden wall $2^1/2 \times 4$ inches / 6.4×10.2 cm **each**
- ❖ Cream pin-stripe for outer border and background $^1/2$ yard / 50 cm
- ❖ Backing / binding 21×21 inches / 53.3×53.3 cm
- ❖ Wadding 20×20 inches / 50.8×50.8 cm
- ❖ Iron-on interfacing $^1/8$ yard / 15 cm

CUTTING INSTRUCTIONS

✂ Templates do not include seam allowances, so remember to add $^1/4$ inch / 6 mm as you cut. All other pattern pieces have seam allowances included in the measurements. Label each pattern piece after it has been cut.

1. Using the appropriate templates, cut one of each of the following pattern pieces: wall (**A**), lower gable (**B**), upper gable (**C**), roof (**D**), hedges (**F1** and **F2**), tree top (**H**), and bushes (**G1** and **G2**). Cut two side hedges (**E**), remembering to reverse one. Cut two birds (**J**) and two birds (**K**) without adding seam allowances because these pieces will be appliquéd using buttonhole stitch.

2. For sides of the house cut one strip, $1 \times 3^1/4$ inches/ 2.5×8.3 cm and one strip, $1 \times 5^1/4$ inches/2.5×13.3 cm.

3. For the chimney, cut a rectangle, $1^1/4 \times 1^1/2$ inches/3.2×3.8 cm.

4. For the door, cut a rectangle, $1^1/2 \times 2^1/2$ inches/3.8×6.4 cm.

5. For the windows, cut two rectangles, $1^1/2 \times 2$ inches/ 3.8×5.1 cm.

6. For the base of the house, cut a strip, $1^1/4 \times 8^1/2$ inches/ 3.2×21.6 cm.

7. For the tree trunk, cut a strip, 1×3 inches/2.5×7.6 cm.

8. For the foreground of the house, cut a rectangle, $2^1/2 \times 14^1/2$ inches/6.4×36.8 cm.

9. For the gate, cut one rectangle, $2 \times 2^1/2$ inches/5.1×6.4 cm and three posts $1/2 \times 2^1/2$ inches/1.3×6.4 cm.

10. For the garden wall, cut 26 'bricks', $1 \times 1^3/4$ inches/ 2.5×4.4 cm from light, medium and dark scraps. Then, cut two brown strips, $1 \times 14^1/2$ inches/2.5×36.8 cm.

11. From the cream pin-stripe fabric, cut a rectangle for the background of the house, 8×15 inches/20.3×38.2 cm. Next, cut two strips, $2^1/2 \times 15$ inches/6.4×38.2 cm, and two strips $2^1/2 \times 19$ inches/6.4×48.2 cm for the outer border.

12. For the 'flower' border, cut 19 rectangles, $1 \times 1^1/4$ inches/ 2.5×3.2 cm from colourful scraps.

13. For the pieced inner border, cut six strips, $1^1/4 \times 10^1/2$ inches/ 3.2×26.7 cm and 30 squares, $1^1/4 \times 1^1/4$ inches/3.2×3.2 cm from an assortment of prints and plaids.

PUTTING THE QUILT TOP TOGETHER

Piece the house unit in the following sequence:

1. Sew the roof (**D**) to the lower gable (**B**). Press open.

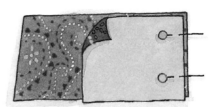

2. Sew the shorter blue stripe post to the left-hand side of the wall (**A**). Press, then sew the two units together. Press.

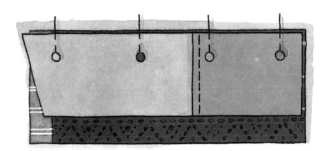

3. Sew the remaining blue stripe post to the right-hand side of the house. Press, then sew a brown strip to the base of the house. Press.

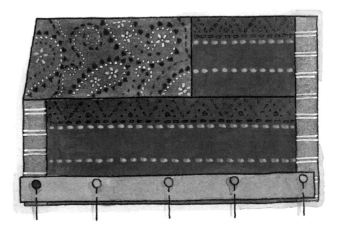

4. Turn under the sloping edges of the upper gable to prepare it for appliqué. With right sides facing, pin, then sew it to the lower gable. Follow the same sequence with the side hedges (**E**).

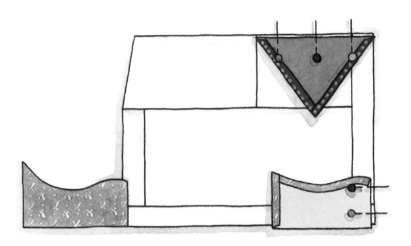

5. Turn under all raw edges of the house unit, then centre and pin it to the cream pin-stripe foundation fabric. The house unit will later be held in place by the quilting.

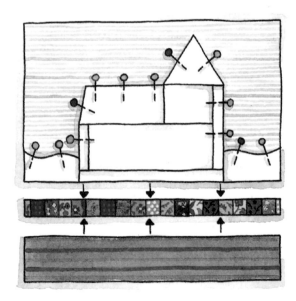

6. Sew the rectangles for the 'flower' border together at random to make a pieced strip, 1 × 14$\frac{1}{2}$ inches / 2.5 × 36.8 cm.

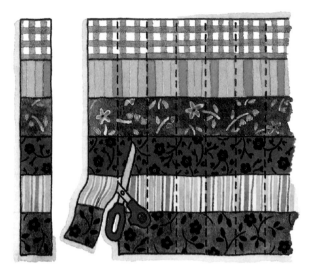

7. Sew the house unit, 'flower' border and brown foreground together as illustrated. Press flat.

8. To make the garden wall, sew two identical rows of 12 'bricks' each, alternating colours. Press seams towards the darker fabric. Pin, then sew the rows together taking care to off-set the blocks to resemble bricks. Trim off the ends so the pieced unit measures 14$\frac{1}{2}$ inches / 36.8 cm.

9. Sew a brown strip to the top and bottom of the brick wall. Press.

10. Join hedges **F1** and **F2** down the centre. Press seam open, then sew the hedge to the brick wall.

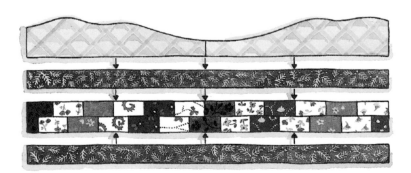

11. Turn under and baste the curved raw edge of the hedge. Pin, then appliqué in place to overlap the foreground of the house.

12. Turn under and baste the raw edges of the following pattern pieces to prepare for appliqué: door, two windows, chimney, tree top and trunk, two bushes, gate and posts. Do not turn under the **bottom** edges of the chimney, tree trunk and bushes as they will be covered by other pieces.

13. Since the birds are awkward shapes to appliqué, press them onto fusible interfacing for easy handling. Cut them out and sew into position using a buttonhole stitch.

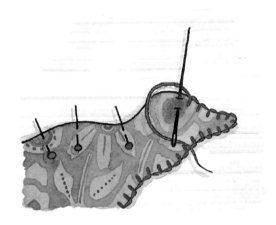

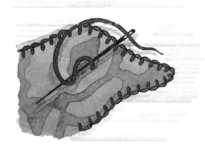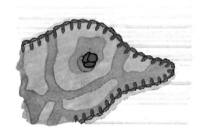

14. Appliqué all prepared shapes, except gate, in position. Slipstitch with a matching thread making very small stitches.

15. To make the gate, appliqué one of the strips diagonally across the striped square, then appliqué the two side posts in position to give the appearance of a gate.

ADDING THE BORDERS

1. Trim the edges of the background square. Measure the sides and top of the quilt to determine the exact measurements required for the pieced inner border.

2. To quick-piece the inner border, first sew together the six $1\frac{1}{4}$ inch / 3.2 cm wide strips. Press all seams in the same direction. Cut the pieced strip at $1\frac{1}{4}$ inch / 3.2 cm intervals to make eight multi-coloured strips.

3. Alternate the assorted $1\frac{1}{4}$ inch / 3.2 cm squares previously cut, along with the multi-coloured strips to make two pieced borders approximately $14\frac{1}{2}$ inches / 36.8 cm long, and two approximately $16\frac{1}{2}$ inches / 41.9 cm long.

4. Pin, then sew the pieced border strips to the sides of the quilt. Press carefully, then sew the pieced borders to the top and bottom. Press again.

5. Pin, then sew the outer border strips following the same sequence.

FINISHING & QUILTING

1. Press the quilt top carefully, and remove all loose threads which may show through to the front.

2. Transfer the quilting patterns according to the quilting plan.

3. Assemble the quilt layers, baste thoroughly and quilt.

4. Trim the wadding even with the raw edges of the quilt top. Trim the backing to extend $\frac{3}{4}$ inch / 1.9 cm beyond the wadding.

5. Use the self-binding method as described in the Techniques section to finish the raw edges of the quilt.

TEMPLATES

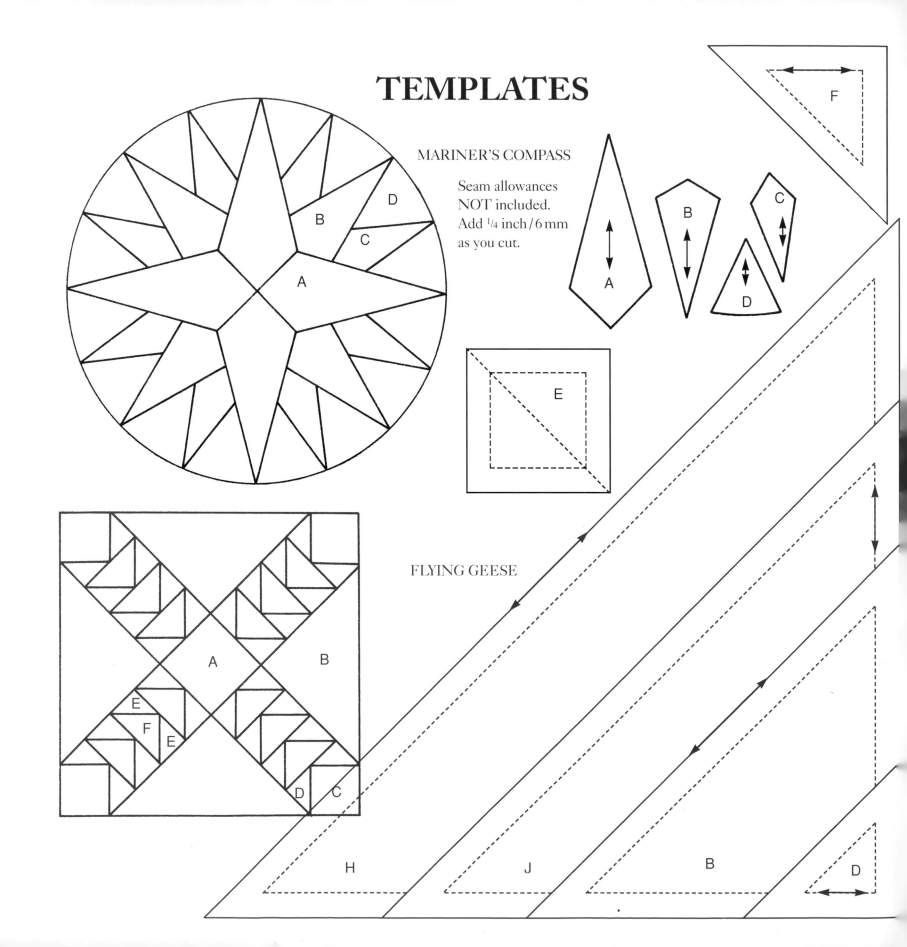

MARINER'S COMPASS

Seam allowances
NOT included.
Add ¼ inch / 6 mm
as you cut.

FLYING GEESE

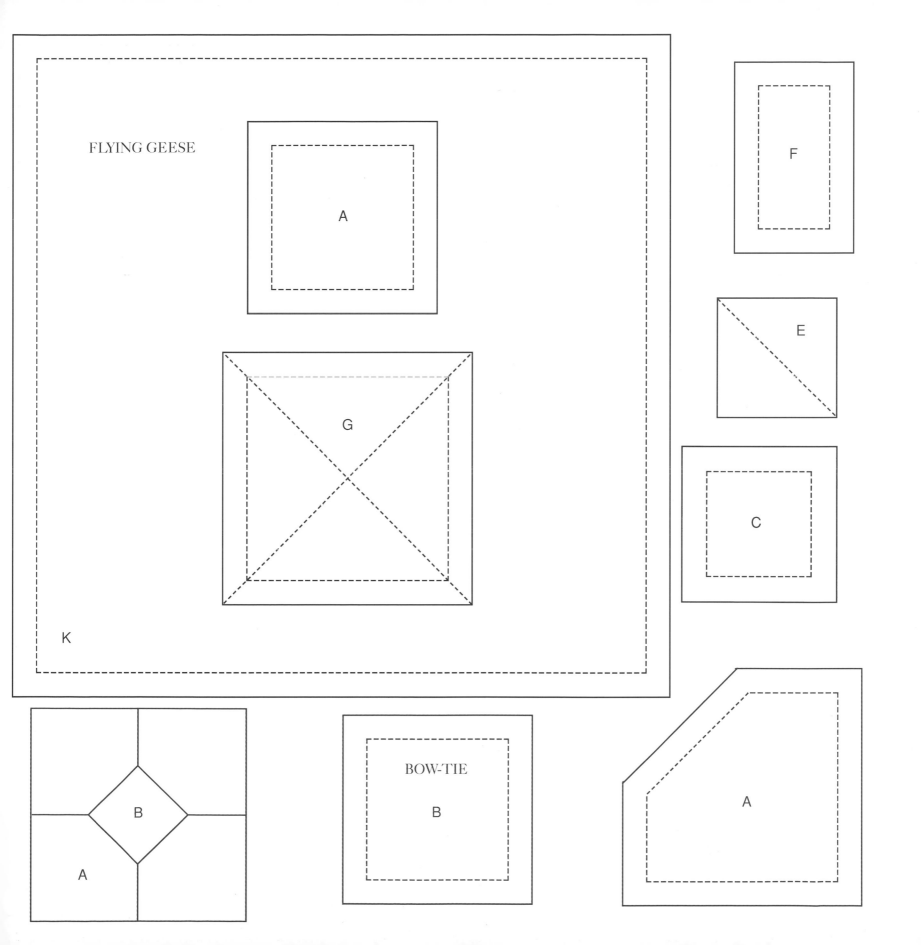

FLYING GEESE

A

G

K

F

E

C

B

A

BOW-TIE

B

A

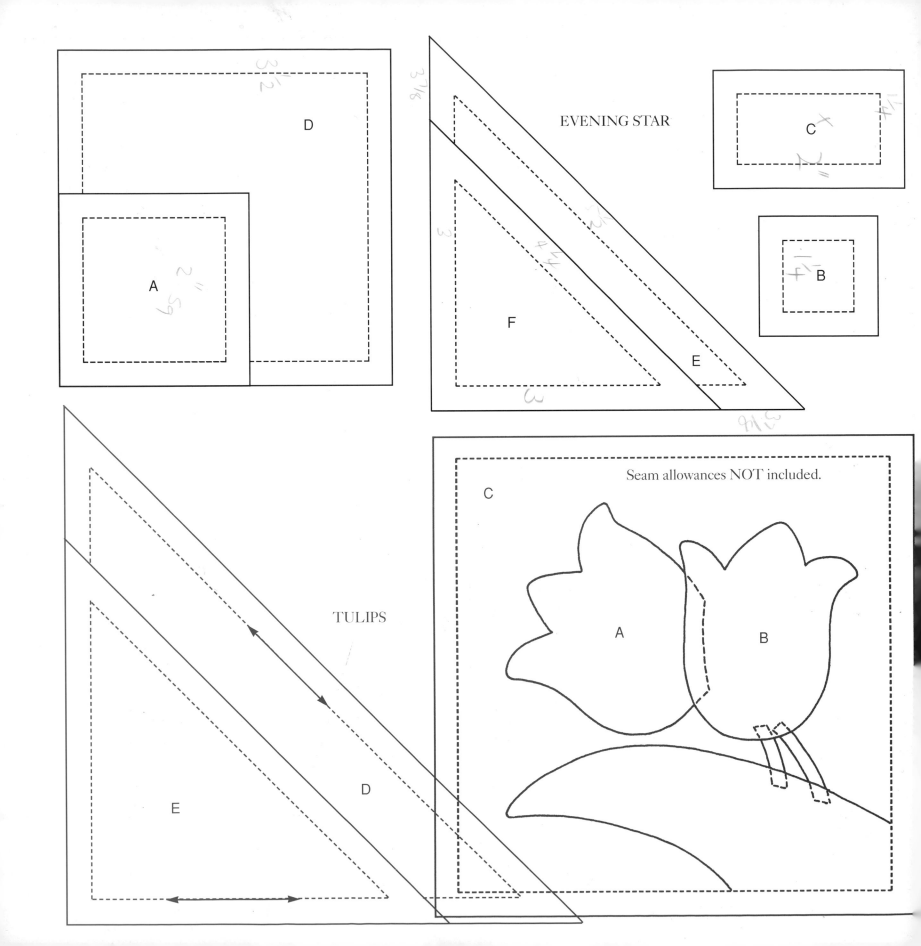

D

3½

A

2"

5/8

EVENING STAR

3⅞

3

4¼

F

3

E

3⅛

C

4¼

2"

B

1¼

1½

TULIPS

E

D

C

Seam allowances NOT included.

A

B

FLOWERPOTS

Seam allowances NOT included.
Add ¼ inch / 6 mm as you cut.

A

D

B

C

BLUEBIRD

B

C

D

E

B

C

A

B

A

PENNSYLVANIA WREATH

B

NINE-PATCH

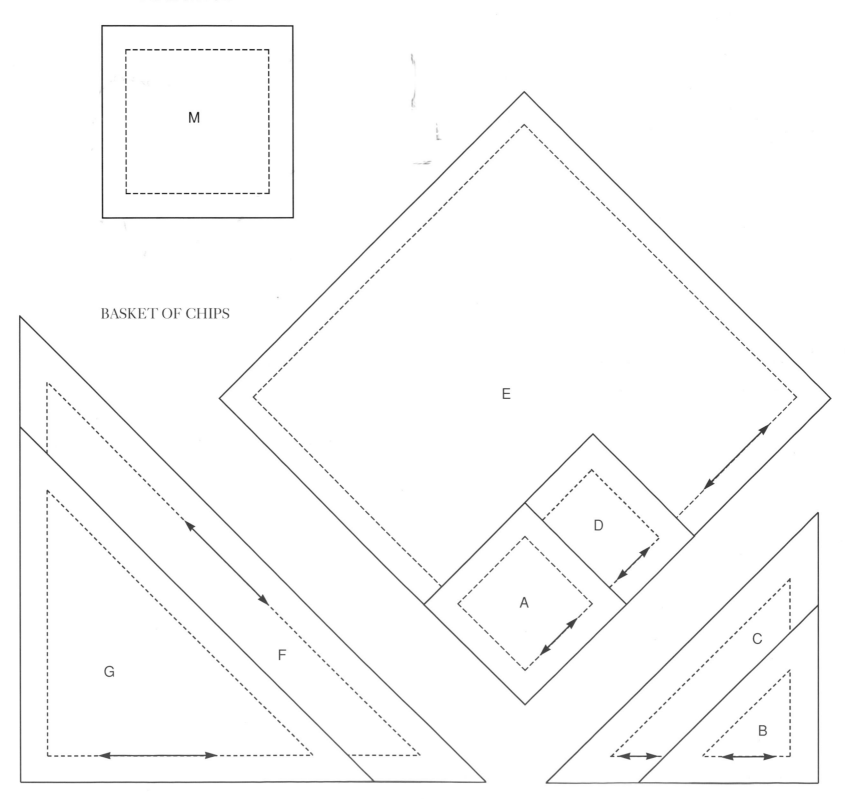

M

BASKET OF CHIPS

E

D

A

C

B

F

G

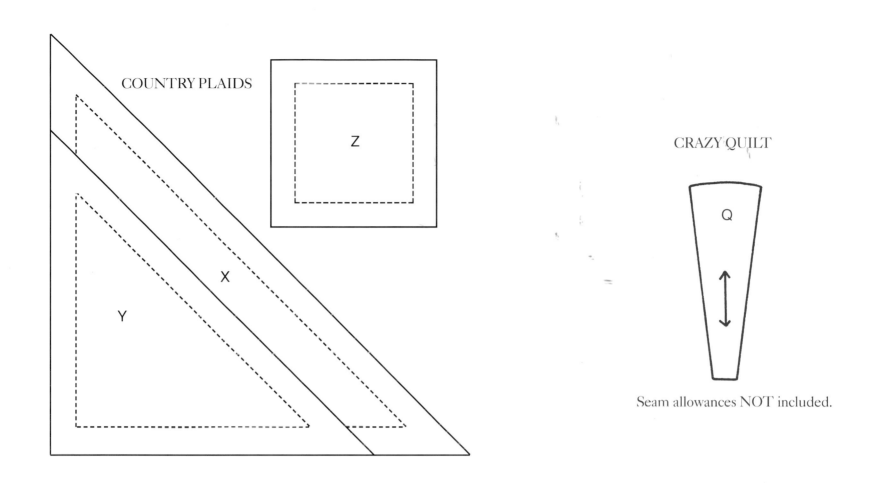

COUNTRY PLAIDS

Z

X

Y

CRAZY QUILT

Q

Seam allowances NOT included.

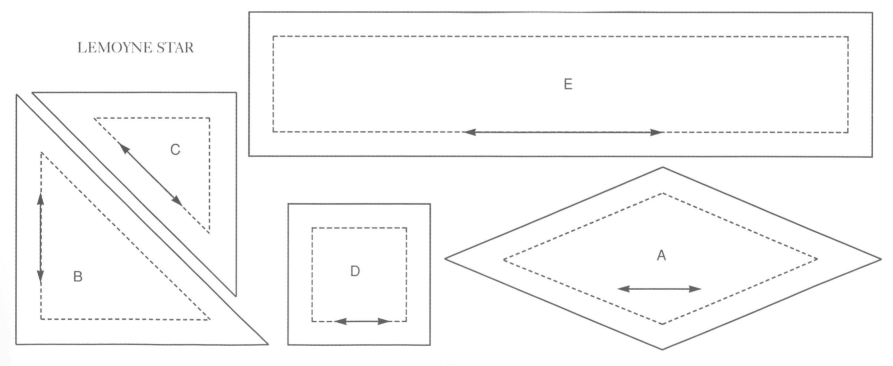

LEMOYNE STAR

E

C

B

D

A

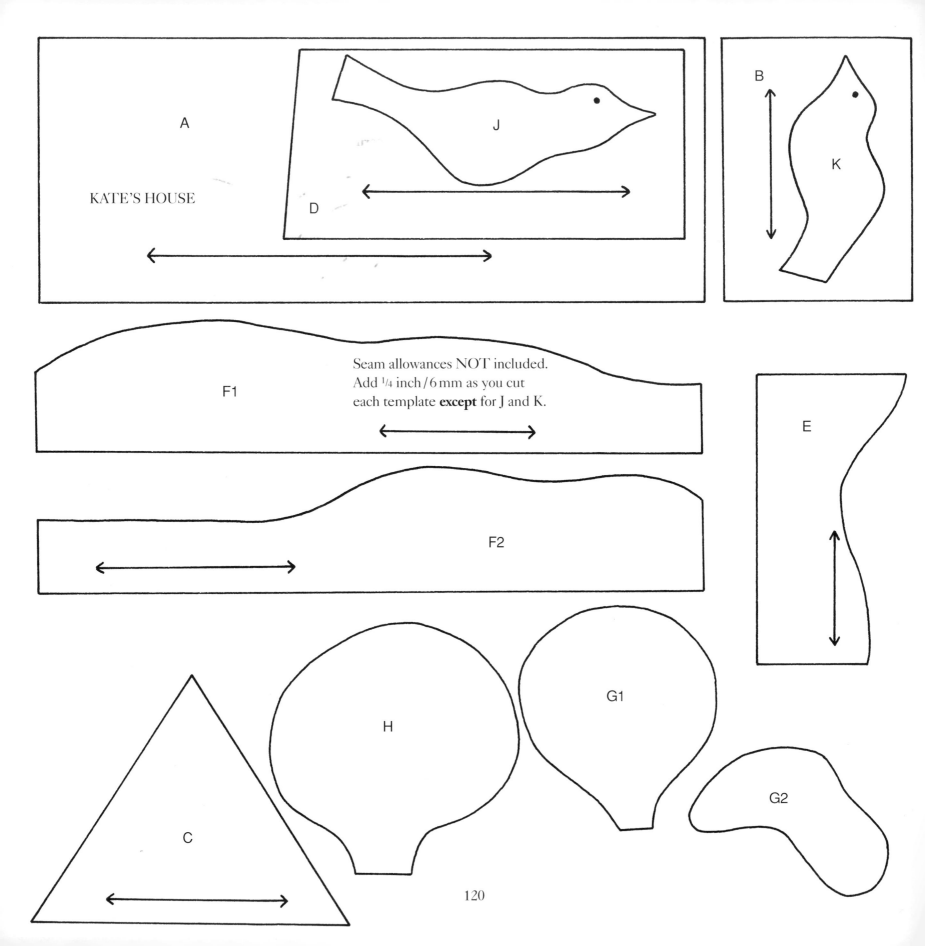

A

KATE'S HOUSE

J

D

B

K

F1

Seam allowances NOT included.
Add ¼ inch / 6 mm as you cut
each template **except** for J and K.

E

F2

C

H

G1

G2

QUILTING PATTERNS

FLYING GEESE

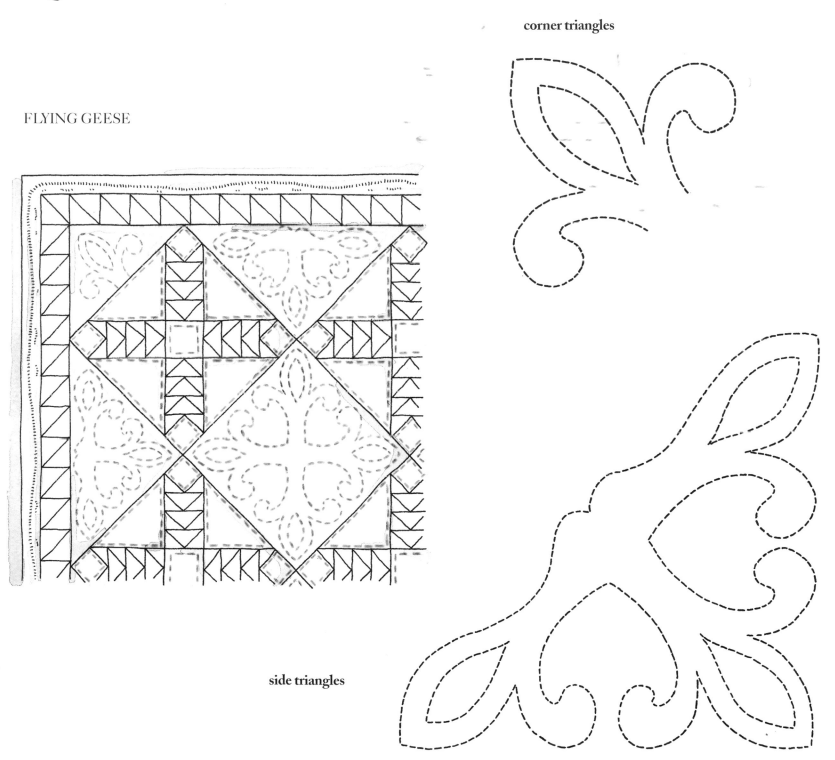

side triangles

FLYING GEESE setting squares

BOW-TIE
border

BOW-TIE

BOW-TIE
corner posts

122

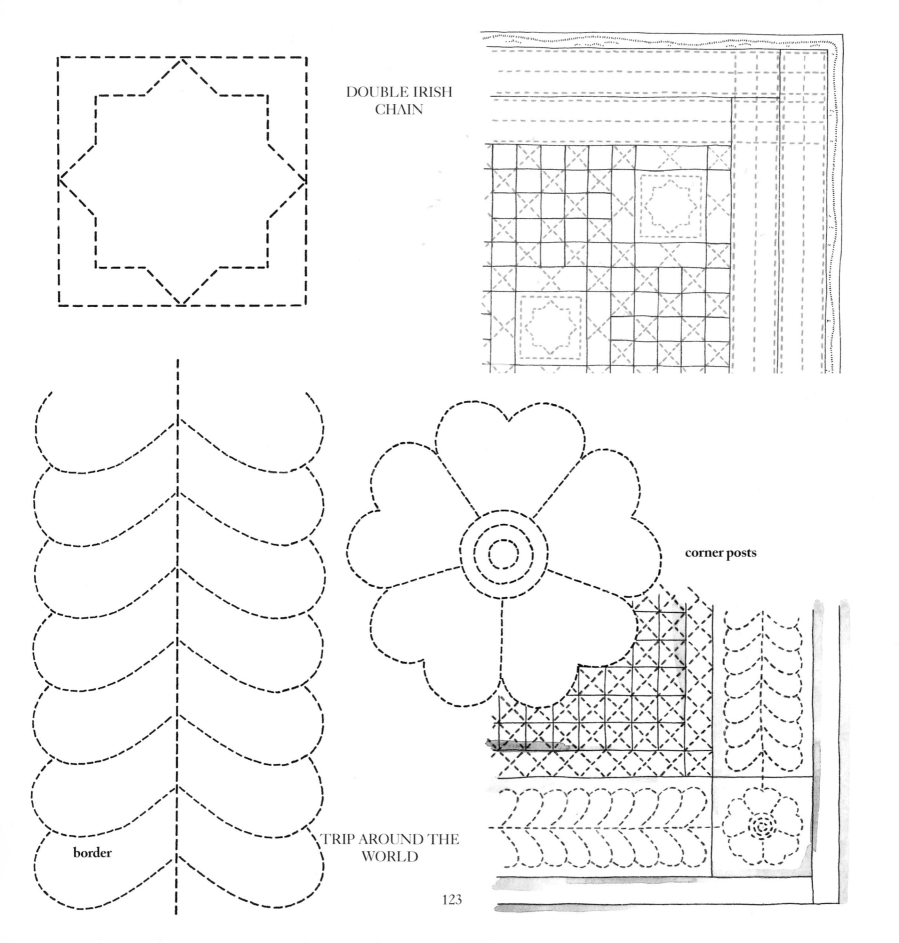

DOUBLE IRISH
CHAIN

corner posts

border

TRIP AROUND THE
WORLD

123

BASKET OF CHIPS

Trace entire pattern for setting squares. Use half of the pattern for the side triangles and a quarter for the corner blocks.

border

124

KATE'S HOUSE

border

125

ACKNOWLEDGEMENTS

I am grateful beyond words to Susan and Gareth Jenkins who offered me the opportunity to write this book and supported me with confidence and optimism. As co-author, Caroline Wilkinson and I shared all the joys and difficulties of this rewarding experience. A thousand thanks to the skilled and enthusiastic quilters who helped piece, appliqué and quilt many of my projects: Karen Scharman for quilting Flowerpots and Basket of Chips, Patricia Hambrick for Flying Geese and Lemoyne Star, Monica Milner for Pennsylvania Wreath, Pat Howarth and Rachel Bell for Tulips, Judith Hammersla for Irish Chain, and Anne Spira for Bow-Tie. A very special thank you to my editors, Ljiljana Ortolja-Baird and Annlee Landman who brought an unerring eye for quality and detail. Penny Brown's illustrations contribute enormous interest and vitality to this book. Her consummate skill at translating my faint sketches into full-blown illustrations is much admired and appreciated. My thanks to Edward Harbour who contributed much to the visual clarity and design of the book. A special thanks to my children, John and Elizabeth, who had the good grace to appear only momentarily astonished when I embarked on this project. And to my husband Denis, the bedrock of my life. His love and support makes everything possible.

Adele Corcoran

I would like to thank Susan Jenkins of Museum Quilts Publications for giving me the opportunity to do this book and for her support and encouragement throughout. I would like to pay a special tribute to my editors, Ljiljana Ortolja-Baird and Annlee Landman for their patience, understanding and advice. I owe a special thanks to Monica Milner for making the Bluebird quilt and to Janice Gunner for quilting Kate's House. I am especially indebted to my co-author Adele Corcoran and we are both extremely grateful to Penny Brown for her wonderful illustrations which give so much to this book. Finally, I would like to thank my family: Michael, Richard and Rupert for their helpful comments and Kate who deserves a very special mention and thanks for her encouragement, constructive criticism and tremendous hard work in typing my manuscript.

Caroline Wilkinson